Move On, Move Up

Move On, Move Up

Turn Yesterday's Trials into Today's Triumphs

PAULA WHITE

New York   Boston   Nashville

Unless otherwise indicated, Scriptures are taken from the King James Version of the Bible.

Scriptures noted *The Message* are taken from *The Message*. Copyright © 1993, 1994, 1995, 1996, 2000, 2001, 2002. Used by permission of NavPress Publishing Group.

Scriptures noted NIV are taken from the HOLY BIBLE, NEW INTERNATIONAL VERSION®. Copyright © 1973, 1978, 1984 by International Bible Society. Used by permission of Zondervan. All rights reserved.

Scriptures noted NKJV are taken from the New King James Version. Copyright © 1982 by Thomas Nelson, Inc.Used by permission. All rights reserved.

Scriptures marked NLT are taken from the Holy Bible, New Living Translation, copyright © 1996, 2004. Used by permission of Tyndale House Publishers, Inc., Wheaton, Illinois 60189. All rights reserved.

FaithWords
Hachette Book Group USA
237 Park Avenue
New York, NY 10017

Visit our Web site at www.faithwords.com.

Printed in the United States of America

First Edition: October 2008
10 9 8 7 6 5 4 3 2 1

FaithWords is a division of Hachette Book Group USA, Inc.
The FaithWords name and logo are trademarks of
Hachette Book Group USA, Inc.

Library of Congress Cataloging-in-Publication Data

White, Paula.
    Move on, move up : turn yesterday's trials into today's triumphs / Paula
White. — 1st ed.
        p. cm.
     ISBN-13: 978-0-446-58045-8 (regular edition)
     ISBN-13: 978-0-446-54133-6 (large print edition)
     ISBN-10: 0-446-58045-7 (regular edition)
     ISBN-10: 0-446-54133-8 (large print edition)   1. Consolation.
  2. Change—Religious aspects—Christianity.   3. Loss (Psychology)—
Religious aspects—Christianity.   4. Self-help techniques. I. Title.
     BV4909.W49 2008
     248.8'6—dc22
                                                          2008017647

To Kristen: The emblem and epitome of beauty and strength.

Contents

Introduction: Shaken, but Still Standing   ix

1   Moving On!   1

2   The Best Thing You Can Do in a Time of Trouble   15

3   Taking Courage in the Crisis Moment   24

4   Look for the "New and Wonderful" in Your Life   40

5   Refuse to Trade in Process for Progress   54

6   Resuming Forward Motion   62

7   How Much of Your Spiritual Mind
Are You Using?   76

8   Develop the Faith That Overcomes Fear   92

9   Back to Your Future   110

10   Cut to the Designer's Pattern   121

11   Refined to Reflect His Glory   131

12   Practical Tactics in Times of Transition   143

13   Validate Your Own Value   165

14   The Makeover You Really Want   180

15 Don't Ask "Why?" Ask "How?"   197

16 Face Your "Issues"   210

17 Dodging the Mudslinging   230

18 The Changing Landscape of Your Path   255

19 Gaining Strength through Perseverance   270

    About the Author   283

Introduction
Shaken, but Still Standing

Several years ago a word was spoken to me by a godly man—a statement I knew was from God. He declared very specifically things the Lord had shown me when I was a young believer.

He then said, "Paula, everything around you that can be shaken is going to be shaken. Things you have counted on as being sure will crumble. But you, Paula, will remain standing and you will emerge with strength."

His bold, direct words with the love of God branded my soul. I had absolutely no doubt that he was speaking truth to me. His message, on the one hand, was not at all what I wanted to hear. On the other hand, his message was not without hope.

In the next few years, his words came to pass. Everything around me that could be shaken was shaken. Things I had counted on as being sure crumbled. But I am still standing, and deep within, I know I am stronger than I have ever been in my faith, my purpose, and my position.

I have known the depths of heartache.

I have also known the even greater depths of God's love and sustaining power.

And I have come to understand the processes of God in a way I have never understood them before.

This is not at all to say that I wanted things around me to be shaken. Far from it!

It is not to say that I have not cried hundreds of buckets of tears. I have. I often say, "I didn't write the script, but I am learning to walk it out with dignity and honor by the grace of God."

As things around me were shaken, and some things around me crumbled in what seemed more like a crash, I spent long hours alone with God — praying, writing in my personal journals, reading the Word of God, and struggling to gain a perspective on what God's purposes might be for the pain I was experiencing.

Some things remain a mystery to me. As long as we are on this earthly side of eternity, we will never have a full answer to all "why" questions.

Other things have become crystal clear. One of the things I have come to see clearly and with certainty is that God creates out of chaos. We often think that creativity happens when all things are in perfect order; however, the opposite is true. The entire cosmos was produced out of a watery, smothering, dark, chaotic nothingness. An empty wasteland.

God creates out of chaos.

No matter how chaotic your life may be, you are precisely in the right position for God to do a creative work!

God speaks His Word to you.

He sheds His light on your situation.

He gives you freedom to breathe in His inspiration and He sets your feet on the solid footing of His truth. He secures you during instability.

He establishes order and rhythm in your life.

He gives you opportunity to become fruitful and to fully embrace and become involved with all things that are for your benefit and fulfillment.

What a Creator!

And what joy that He calls us to participate fully in His creative processes.

All of God's plans and purposes for your life are *good*. They were good at the moment of your creation. They are good today. They will always be good and cannot be anything other than good because they are the work of a totally good and holy God.

The bad things you have experienced may have dented or tarnished or sullied the outer person that you are. Your flesh may have been hit and scars may remain. God hasn't changed His mind about you. He still longs to be in a relationship with you. He still has a good plan and purpose for you. The key to not only moving on but moving up is this: God has a process for your perfection.

The key to not only moving on but moving up is this:
God has a process for your perfection.

God's process is directed toward your having, doing, and being *everything* God says you can have, do, and be.

God's process is presented to us in God's Word, and it is a process available to every person who will seek to discover it, embrace it, and persevere in it.

For most people, the recognition of God's process begins at a point of pain or difficulty. In anguish and devastation a person wants to move on, but she doesn't know how. And she wants to move up—she senses there is more, but she doesn't know where to find it. She wants out of the current circumstances—and especially out of the current pain—but she is unsure which direction to move or where to turn. She knows that she did not intend her life story to contain certain chapters that life has been writing. She does not know how to place the chapter or life event that she struggles to accept—much less understand the whys of—in context with the overall story. I understand; I have been there.

That's what this book is all about.

It's about aligning your life with God's processes so you can experience God's perfection, and in experiencing the fullness of God's plan, experience all that will give you meaning and purpose. I am not saying, "I have arrived"; it is a continual journey. However, I do know something about being processed and learning to stay in position for the purpose of God.

I invite you to the process...and to the fulfillment of your life. As you find this fulfillment, you may be shaken—but you will always stand in victory. You will move on, and you will move up!

Move
On,
Move
Up

1

Moving On!

Patricia stood in silence on the small plot of ground where her home had once been located. She stared with vacant eyes at the gnarled trees across the dirt road, trying to remember the details of what had once been there. The storm that had passed through the area nearly four years earlier had destroyed most of her community. In a matter of minutes all that had been familiar and comfortable was reduced to rubble. Hearts were devastated as family members had separated in their search for survival and neighbors had said good-bye to neighbors, perhaps for the last time in their lives.

Builders were coming in the morning to lay new foundations for Patricia and two of her former neighbors. Her family members were excited. Patricia had not fully sorted out her emotions. She was still angry at the unseen forces that had ripped her life apart. She was still in grief at her loss. She was still perplexed, wondering if there was any purpose in all that had happened, other than a renewed awareness of a fickle and uncontrollable cosmos. She mostly felt numb.

"It's been four years," Patricia's daughter had said. "It's time to build again, Mom."

Patricia wanted to share her daughter's enthusiasm, but she saw nothing ahead aside from hard work and struggle. The past was still too vivid and too raw for her to feel much hope.

Thousands of miles away...

Ubara stood in the doorway of her house staring down the roadway to the east, her eyes focused and penetrating. She longed for nothing but to see her two sons walk out of the dense foliage where the road took a turn and seemed to end several hundred yards away. It had been eight months since renegade military extremists had taken her two sons at gunpoint, conscripting them into a political struggle that Ubara knew little and cared nothing about. She had seen fear in the eyes of her sons, but any thought of defying the crazed and angry soldiers would have been suicidal.

Most of Ubara's neighbors had told her they thought, by now, her sons must certainly be dead or they would have returned. A few held out some hope that her sons were still alive, conjecturing that her sons could be working in the capital city so they might bring home money. One neighbor thought her sons might be reluctant to return in order to protect Ubara.

In recent days, Ubara's husband and married daughter had told her that it was time for her to resume the full extent of her chores and responsibilities. She knew she had neglected her husband during the last few months. She had been spending more and more time standing at the doorway. It seemed now that she alone held out full hope and longing that her sons would return—and that it would be only by the force of her will and desire that they would reappear and make her heart, and family, whole again.

She had asked, "Why my sons?" a thousand times.

She had cried, "I didn't deserve this. I have been a good wife and mother." She believed what she said with all her heart.

She had wondered, *What will happen next?* She dared not think about the worst, even as she also dared not think that life could or might move forward without her sons.

How could she resume full responsibility for her chores? How could she regain full engagement with her husband and daughter, son-in-law, and grandchildren? How might she once again be the joyful and teasing Ubara her family and friends tell her she used to be? These questions had no answers.

Still thousands more miles away...

Styrle stood, with a tall latte cupped in both hands, staring out the window of her eighteen-story condominium. The vast expanse of a wintry Lake Michigan stretched before her. She had only a few moments before she needed to take the elevator down to the walkway that bridged to her office and there begin the twelve-hour day that forced her to give full emotional and mental focus to the management tasks of her company. She was grateful she didn't have any more "spare moments." Those that she did have seemed always to gravitate back to the fact that her husband was gone. Physically, he had moved out of the condo five months before. Emotionally and sexually, he had moved completely out of their marriage more than a year ago.

Styrle missed the smell of her former husband's aftershave, the sound of his laughter as he watched old Groucho Marx television shows, and the way he had once looked at her—many years ago—with appreciation and affection. She did not miss the cold, aloof, silent man he had become. She had many questions about how the warm and fun-loving man she had married fifteen years ago had turned into the cold and rigid man who had sat across the table, flanked by attorneys, as they wrangled about portfolio division and property disposition.

On the one hand, she blamed their divorce on their mutual-but-separate success. Both of them had started their own businesses, which they in turn had taken to the top. On the other hand, she blamed the "age in which we live"—too many temptations and too high a set of expectations for perfection. In her heart of hearts, she truly did not know what more she might have done to keep her husband focused on and faithful to her. Even so, she felt she had failed in some way—certainly in her own eyes, also in the eyes of her parents and siblings, and ultimately before God. Divorce was never something she had expected to happen in her life.

Even though the final divorce pronouncement had been recent, Styrle's friends knew the estrangement had been progressing for years and they were already encouraging her to get on with her life. Two of her friends had told her only the day before she should make herself available for dating again, and one of the women had even made a suggestion or two about eligible men she might invite to a dinner party.

Styrle cringed at the thought. From her perspective, the ink on the divorce decree was barely dry. Furthermore, how could she trust again? How could she love again? She wasn't at all sure how much she would be able to risk her own emotions to future rejection.

"It's time to get back on the playing field," one of her friends had said.

"You've got to get out there!" another friend advised.

She found herself thinking about their statements that morning as she stared out her window. *What playing field? Is it all a game? Out where?* And even more important, she questioned, *Why?*

I have felt what each of these women has felt. I've been there, too—engulfed in a painful past and not knowing how to move forward in a positive way.

I lived a wonderful life as a little girl. My father was my superhero. Every morning, Daddy took me to breakfast and let me order whatever I wanted, and just to make it extra-special, he drew a smiley face on my pancakes with syrup. After breakfast we would go to the country club, where Daddy and his friends laughed and drank heartily, played cards, and gambled in smoke-filled rooms. I had the run of the club and created all kinds of mischief, but I was Daddy's girl so nobody stopped me.

From the club we'd often go to the toy store my parents owned and my mother managed. I'd scoop up all the toys I could hold, and Mom would say I couldn't keep them, but Daddy always said I could. And Daddy always won. Sometimes he'd even take me to the park after that, and then we'd end up back at the house, watching our favorite TV shows, drinking V-8 juice together, and resting on the couch. I felt like the luckiest girl in the world.

Then the horrible night came when my father showed up at our front door drunk and demanded that I be handed over to him. My mother refused, and they literally had a tug-of-war fight, each of them holding one of my arms. For the first time I saw my father become violent, and in the end, the police came and took Daddy away. He was released from their custody some time later, but in a disoriented state, my father killed himself just as he had vowed to do if he couldn't have me with him.

For decades, my little-girl reactions to Daddy's suicide echoed through my mind: *How do I wake up from this nightmare? All I want is to be held and cuddled, feel safe, and be loved!*

Nothing added up. Daddy loved me—how could he leave me? What about me was so unlovable?

After Daddy died, our situation changed dramatically. My father's family took over all the family businesses as my mother chose to move forward with her life. Mother worked long hours to support my older brother and me, and I hardly ever saw her. She arranged for a lot of babysitters—teenaged girls and boys from the neighborhood. They were supposed to take care of me. But I was just six years old when a babysitter began to violate me. Over the weeks and years that followed, it happened over and over. I'd run and hide for hours afterward thinking about what a bad girl I must be. I'd take long baths to try to get clean again, and I'd cry as I sat in the bathtub, pleading with the world, *Will someone please love me?*

I strove for perfection, trying to make myself lovable. I studied hard to be a straight-A student, a trophy-winning gymnast, a diligent worker, and an attractive, thin girl—surely such a girl could be loved! To stay skinny as I entered my teen years, I began to purge and exercise even harder. I struggled with eating disorders for seven years.

In my anger over my father's death, I began to manipulate my mother and others—friends, teachers, and any counselor who tried to help me confront my problems. All the while, I continued my frantic search for someone to fill the void that the loss of my daddy had left in my heart. I went from boyfriend to boyfriend—and with each broken relationship, the hollowness in the pit of my stomach grew deeper.

One day I was sitting in the home of an older woman and her middle-aged son. As we sat around the table, we talked about various things, and then suddenly this man said to me, "I have the answers to your problems and the solution to your pain." Initially I was defensive and didn't want to hear what he had to say. But as I felt his sincerity and love, I let down my defenses and began to receive from him.

He pulled out a book that had the words "Holy Bible" printed on the front of it. He read to me from that book and told me about Jesus. It was the first time I had ever heard anything about Jesus or encountered the Bible. It may be hard for you to believe that a seventeen-year-old girl living in a southern state of the United States of America had never heard the story of Jesus or the words of the Bible—but it was true. This man prayed with me and before night fell, I had accepted Jesus Christ, the living Son of God, as my personal Lord and Savior. It was the most glorious day of my life. I knew without a doubt, deep in my spirit, *I was loved!*

I was not, however, emotionally healed of my past on that day. For years—even after I was involved in full-time ministry—I struggled periodically with roller-coaster emotions that were deeply rooted in my father's suicide and the abuse I had experienced as a young girl. Just when I seemed to make some progress and move forward, I was knocked back again. Old feelings and memories consumed my mind. Even as I smiled on the outside and helped others who had been abused, I was overwhelmed with anger at those who had hurt me.

Would I ever get beyond this?

I knew I needed to...but how? What would it take for me to be able to step into a bright, loving future that wasn't haunted by a horribly abusive and devastatingly sorrowful past?

WHAT IT MEANS TO MOVE ON

Although their circumstances are very different, each of the three women I described earlier faces what millions of people around the world face today—the challenge of "moving on" from the past, and moving toward a future that has not been clearly defined and is far from secure and discernable.

Move on?

There's far more to moving on than getting out of bed and putting one foot in front of the next—although that certainly is a starting point for some people.

Moving on means making new plans, taking on the future, and redefining what needs to be redefined. It means understanding and ultimately accepting that the landscape of your life has changed.

Moving on means making new plans, taking on the future, and redefining what needs to be redefined.

In many cases, moving on means moving out of the past—literally, at times, and emotionally, at times, and ultimately in most cases, both. Moving on means sorting through the past, gleaning the best from it, and reaching out toward something or someone new. New, of course, can be very exciting. It can also be very scary.

Moving on *can* be a factor related to sheer survival.

Moving on *can* be an outgrowth of rebellion.

Moving on *can* be a healthy embracing of growth and an opportunity for personal development.

Moving on, in all cases, means some degree of *change*.

To change means to make or become different. To make an alteration or modification. A new experience. Although change is unavoidable on this journey of life, it can be difficult to embrace. The reason is that all change and transition initially feel like loss. How do we embrace an unknown future and leave a familiar past? This can be challenging and costly if not maneuvered carefully.

Yes, by all means, *move on.*

But the challenge to move on is not only for the Patricias, Ubaras, and Styrles of this world. It is the challenge facing every person…at some point and often at all times.

Why?

Because change is inevitable. The only thing constant in life is change!

The question is not, *Are things changing?* but rather, *How am I dealing with change? How am I receiving, responding to, and reacting to change?*

Are you a willing participant in the change process? Or are you kicking and screaming against the forces of change that are beyond your control?

MOVING ON IS A PROCESS

I encourage you to think of "move on" as a *process* phrase. The truth is, we are all in process, all the time. God has designed us for growth and development, from the moment of our conception until the moment of death. We may not be growing and developing physically every minute of every year, but we are changing physically—and ideally, we are growing and developing emotionally, mentally, and spiritually every day of our lives. That's the design. That's the plan. Ultimately the individual purpose of growth is to produce the character of God in our lives.

We have the choice of embracing growth and development or attempting to deny, thwart, or redirect it. As much as we try, however, we can never completely sidestep or control change.

We have the choice of embracing growth and development or attempting to deny, thwart, or redirect it.

I certainly am aware of many of the health books that attempt to defy aging, and I also am highly in favor of living a high-quality, healthy, productive, and energetic life for as long as possible. Even so, aging occurs and death comes. That's the inevitable fact of life. Instead of living in a form of denial and questioning why one dies, the better choice is to embrace the realities of life and ask why one was born.

We need to accept what is inevitable and uncontrollable—and then seek to exert influence over all other factors.

Between birth and death, we can do countless things to direct and control change, and even some things to control the rate of change in our lives, but we can never completely stop change. Growth is optional; change is mandatory. It happens! We each face three challenges when it comes to change, and whether we meet them determines whether we move *up* as well as *on*. The challenges are to pursue *positive* change, to seek *meaningful* change, and to put together a chain of *sequential and cumulative* changes that build a better life.

Pursuing Positive Change

The alternative to positive change is to slip and slide through life according to circumstances. If a person allows circumstances to direct her life, there's a high probability those circumstances are negative, and if so, they are likely to direct her life toward negative outcomes.

For example, the death of a spouse can be devastating. What might be done in the aftermath of experiencing such a negative circumstance? Some widows give up—their lives become increasingly narrow and unproductive. They see a significant part of their reason for being as having been stripped from them, and they have great difficulty in making new friendships or trying new things. Some suffer financially because they have not trained themselves in money management or sought to become informed about their family finances. These women become confused about how to handle the money and property they inherit.

In sharp contrast are those widows who pursue new futures. This does not mean they mourn their husbands any less. It means, rather, that they refuse to become paralyzed by their losses. They are willing to make changes, consider a full range of options, and then pursue what they believe will give them the greatest opportunity for meaningful and positive lives.

In some cases, they devote more of their time and energy to their own creative passions or intellectual interests. Sometimes they dive into volunteer work and faith-based ministries. Going back to school to study things that have long been of interest can finally become possible for them. Or perhaps they give the deposit of wealth stored within their souls through time and experience to younger people still trying to figure out who they are and what life's about.

A meaningful and positive future does not *automatically* flow from a negative circumstance—but the good news is that an unproductive and negative future is not an automatic outcome from a negative circumstance. A person must choose to recognize that the process of change is in effect and then choose to pursue positive growth.

Seeking Meaningful Change

Change just for the sake of change profits little. We must seek not only positive change but change that is meaningful and purpose filled. In times marked by difficult circumstances it is too easy to make quick, seemingly easy, overly optimistic changes in the hopes that *anything* will be better than what is. That isn't the case.

We must seek not only positive change but change that is meaningful and purpose filled.

The newly divorced person who jumps into another marriage within weeks...the person who is fired from a company and immediately goes to work for a competitor with a spirit of revenge in her heart...or the widow who quickly discards all of her husband's belongings and moves to Florida even though she cannot tolerate heat or humidity...are examples of change not rooted in positive and meaningful purpose.

In the embracing of change, we must be certain we are making choices and decisions that truly have the potential for giving us greater fulfillment and deeper inner satisfaction. We must make changes that further the release of our God-given potential, not just changes that offer a quick fix of money, fame, or affection.

Seeking Sequential and Cumulative Change

Positive and meaningful change has a cumulative effect. God's Word tells us that the good things in our lives can grow exponentially, so that we move from "grace to grace" and from "glory to glory." That means we *build* upon our successes. We develop our talents and skills to their highest level and use them in ways that attract future opportunity. It means we begin to see patterns in our lives that enable us to put the pieces together into a greater and greater whole.

The alternative is to hopscotch through our lives, jumping from one seemingly good idea to the next, from one relationship to the next, from one opportunity to the next, never landing long enough to get accurate bearings about where we may be headed, or why we are making the moves we make.

Virtually all things of quality and lasting value take time to create or build. A person may appear to be an overnight wonder, but in all likelihood if the success is genuine it has been hard earned. It takes a lifetime to build a reputation that goes down in history.

Moving on successfully, therefore, means pursuing positive and meaningful changes that sequentially and cumulatively build a life of quality and purpose. The motion is forward. The result is growth that is fruitful.

This isn't just moving on—it is *moving up!*

From that perspective, what presently is becomes something much greater, grander, and more glorious!

HOW HIGH IS GOD'S HIGH?

I have never met a person who said, "If I won the lottery, I'd decline my winnings." The exact opposite is true—most people want to experience a financial windfall. People want instant miracles and overnight fame and to be catapulted into the arms of a dream lover.

Everybody wants to trade in the ghetto for a penthouse, get to the top of the ladder, or walk the red carpet and be handed the big trophy. Now, not everybody truly believes that he or she can or will experience life at the top, but people nevertheless daydream about or wish for more. The poor want more, the rich want more.

While change is inevitable, moving up is *never* inevitable. It requires intentional choices and decisions.

The examples I have listed are examples about ambitions and desires rooted in human nature. We tend to ask ourselves, *How much do I want? How much do I think I can earn...or have...or achieve...or accomplish?* Those are questions rooted in our own human understanding of our potential and abilities.

But how high is God's high? How good is God's good? How much is in God's storehouse with your name on it?

I am 100 percent convinced that God's high has no ceiling that we human beings can fully fathom. God's best is perfection, completion. God does not deal in "too much" or "too great." God's plan for every person is rooted in words such as "exceedingly," "abundantly," and "more than a person can imagine."

*God's high has no ceiling that we human beings
can fully fathom.*

God's intention is that we move up...but even more so, that we move up to the ever-increasing levels that are according to His plan and purpose.

Keep reading...I'll show you how.

MOVING ON

How do you feel about the idea of moving on in your life?

MOVING UP

What more do you intuitively sense God has for you that you aren't currently experiencing, doing, or displaying in your character or spiritual life?

2

The Best Thing You Can Do
in a Time of Trouble

Danielle's friends found her curled up in her bed at three o'clock in the afternoon. She was not exactly in a fetal position, but she definitely was in hiding. The drapes were closed, the room lit only by the glow of a nightlight. She admitted to her friends that she was trying to escape the demands of her life, and fortunately, she also admitted to them that she couldn't recall how many of the sleeping tablets she had taken from the open bottle on her nightstand.

The friends rushed Danielle to the hospital, where she received emergency treatment for a potential overdose, and then the hospital referred her to a psychiatric hospital for evaluation.

Danielle had not personally experienced horrendous problems, but she had been attempting to help nearly a dozen people close to her who were in serious crises of some type. One had a niece who had experienced a brain aneurysm and remained in a comatose state after surviving a risky surgery. She was given only a 10 percent chance to live. Another friend was dealing with a mother-in-law in intensive care in what physicians were calling a "near vegetative state," and trying to help her husband make wise decisions regarding life-sustaining procedures. The issue was complicated by the fact that the mother-in-law had always positioned herself as an enemy to this friend, who was now feeling that her husband did not trust her judgment to be without vengeance. A third friend was dealing with a stage-three breast cancer diagnosis, a fourth was dealing with a daughter who did not want to be pregnant and was contemplating abortion, and the fifth was dealing with news that her boyfriend had been seen at a party with another woman. And so it went.

The therapists at the mental hospital told Danielle that she was suffering from "over care." She had taken on the personal pain of too many other people to the point that she, too, was experiencing deep inner anguish. While caring is good, we are not designed to carry the full weight of responsibilities for those we love and have compassion for. Danielle admitted to her Christian therapist and to her friends that she had started to question whether God truly loves every person and whether God always plays fair. Not only was Danielle in emotional pain, she was in a faith crisis.

NOBODY IS IMMUNE

Danielle is not the exception in our world. There are millions of people like her, and like her friends. There are seasons in which we face trauma.

Every person I know is experiencing or has experienced some type of pain, trouble, or difficulty in life—not just some of the time, but at any given time! I have heard it said that everybody has a problem, is a problem, or lives with a problem. The same is true for pain and trials. If we are not personally experiencing a time of difficulty, in all likelihood somebody we love is.

That is not being pessimistic but realistic about the ebbs and flows in life. Yes, there are sunny days, but there are also rainy days. Both are a part of the seasons of life, and they have their own distinct purposes. Trouble is not prejudiced. It comes in diverse manifestations and does not discriminate in its visitation. Problems are a part of life. It is also part of life to — if you choose — find resolution and growth in the challenges you face.

As I said earlier, it is not about what you go through, but how you go through it. How does trouble impact you? Yes, pain and problems are part of life, but so are purpose and promise.

Pain and problems are part of life, but so are purpose and promise.

Sometimes the trouble or pain is physical — often related to an injury or a disease, sometimes related to exhaustion or depletion of certain nutrients in the body.

Sometimes the trouble or pain is emotional — the hurt of rejection, criticism, false accusations, prejudice, abuse, or hatred; or perhaps deep sorrow over a divorce, death, or loss of a relationship. Sometimes the anguish involves the sickness, sin, or rebellion of a person who is beloved.

Sometimes the trouble or pain is mental — perhaps mental exhaustion over a problem that can't seem to be resolved, a situation that seems to have no definitive answer, or a dilemma that seems to have no good choices.

Sometimes the trouble or pain is spiritual — guilt or shame associated with sin, or feelings of failing God in some way.

The sources of pain are countless, and usually very personal. But pain can be debilitating or developing to you.

When we are hurt, we often lose sight of the fact that others around us also hurt or have gone through a similar situation. Sometimes their pain is directly related to us, or to the pain we are experiencing. In most cases, it is unique to their own situations and experiences. How we deal with and respond to our trying times either inspires or discourages others who are also hurting or have been hurt.

This book is not a study on pain or problems. Rather, it is a call for you to recognize that you will share a commonality of hurt, wounds, pain, trouble, and trauma with countless other people. You are a spirit being having a human experience. God has provided solutions for all your problems. However, you can never conquer what you don't confront and you cannot confront what you don't identify.

When you are honest and transparent about this, and especially as you can share what you are learning from your pain and problems or ways in which God has helped you in it, you have a great possibility for deeper relationships, spiritual ministry, and purposeful living. Don't waste your trial. Don't fail to move on or move up.

The best thing you can do with your trouble, trial, or pain is this:

Face it, give it to God, and heal.

RECOGNIZING FOUR TRUTHS
ABOUT A TIME OF TRIAL

I do not claim to be an expert, but I do know four essential truths about a time of trial. Those who enter into a time of trial, trouble, or pain need to confront these truths squarely.

1. Denial Doesn't Work

First, there is no advantage in denying emotional pain or attempting to hide a time of trial completely from others. We don't like others to see our weak or wounded areas, for fear of rejection. If we deny a problem, we usually stuff it deep within our souls. The problem festers and brews there until it one day erupts into rage, hate, depression, or vengeance. Trying to hide pain completely from others can make us develop hard veneers over our souls. Such a veneer is always, at least to a certain degree, a lie. Nothing about stuffing a problem or developing a false veneer is productive or beneficial to a person over the long term of his or her life. And it is certainly not in the place of authenticity I encourage you to reach.

Sometimes a person's emotional or spiritual pain reaches the point of being almost invisible, yet the person continues to know that something deep within isn't quite right. The surface emotions might be tension, uneasiness, frustration, stress, or anxiety. But it's likely that the person is in pain at a deep level. This pain is probably related to experiences that occurred many years ago and caused rejection, shame, anger, bitterness, and even hatred that have seethed in the person's subconscious. If you are experiencing what I call "constant, low-grade tension" in life, dig deep into your own heart and mind. Bring your feelings and the experiences related to them to the surface where they can be faced squarely, given to God, and healed. I call it "locating." It is to find and face everything that holds you back from living a full life. Remember, feelings are just that... they are your feelings. They have personal ownership and validity to the person feeling or experiencing them.

2. Pain Begets Pain

Second, anytime we experience pain or trouble in one area of our lives, we are much more prone to trouble and pain in other areas of our lives. You have heard the old saying, "When it rains, it pours." There is a law of interrelated reality. That is where one affects the whole and the whole affects the one principal.

For example, dealing with long-term physical pain can become emotionally exhausting. Long-term emotional pain can lead to spiritual pain. Financial troubles can produce both emotional and relational pain. The total effects of pain are cumulative to the point where some people have difficulty isolating the real sources of their pain. This is where identifying your feelings, discovering what is causing your low-grade tension, can be complicated because they often have multiple layers.

A number of years ago behavioral-science researchers published a chart of "stress points." Their research had revealed that some experiences in life are more stressful than others. I am not aware of a chart of "pain points," but I feel certain one could be readily compiled. Such a chart would need to be highly personal since we each have different definitions for what is difficult or painful. Even so, the truth for all people is that "pain points" can accumulate in people's lives to the point that their overall pain-and-trouble scores are exceedingly high. Be aware that pain can multiply to the point of being nearly unbearable. This can become the breaking point where you are overwhelmed and incapacitated.

3. Pain and Frustration Reveal Change Is Occurring

Third, pain and frustration are oftentimes two of the foremost hallmarks of transition. Very few changes occur without some degree of frustration and agitation—often marked by confusion, tension, and anxiety—and change is frequently interpreted as painful.

We see this clearly in childbirth. A woman can have a trouble-free pregnancy with little physical discomfort, until the time comes for birth. When labor begins, pain occurs. The baby is in transition, and so is the mother. It is the most difficult part of bringing forth this beautiful blessing. Along with the pain, many women feel almost overwhelmed at the new responsibilities, anxieties, and unknowns associated with motherhood. Everything in life will change. The fear of the unknown can be overwhelming.

Transition is the hallway of nowhere between two significant somewheres: where you have already been and where you are going. As I said in the last chapter, change is difficult to embrace because it almost always feels like loss. Growth always involves leaving something behind and learning how to receive, adapt to, grow into, or fully possess something new.

In many cases—perhaps most cases—pain and ongoing frustration are symptoms of a deeper issue that needs resolution and healing. We must always seek to be healed and made whole. Living with tension, anxiety, worry, and hurt is not God's best plan for us. These emotions are signals that something needs to be stopped, started, or altered—now!

Pain and ongoing frustration are symptoms of a deeper issue that needs resolution and healing.

Pain and frustration are often God's way of getting our attention so we will submit to the full processing He desires for our lives. God's intent is never to leave us where we are in a place of hurt but rather to move us to a higher, better, and more fulfilling place and purpose. He takes us from bad situations to better situations, and even from good situations to great situations. He really does have a better future for you if you are willing to walk through the process.

4. We Can Prolong or Shorten the Pain

Fourth, the way in which we respond to trouble and pain determines to a great extent both the longevity and the severity of the difficulty. Never assume that things will get better with no intervention on your part. They certainly will not get better without God's intervention. You must do your part and let God do His part.

Never assume that things will get better with no intervention on your part.

FACE IT—AND GIVE IT TO GOD!

We can fuss and fume and talk about our pain and our problem ad infinitum. But there comes a point when we have to face what is happening and take it to God and say: "Here I am. I hurt. I'm frustrated. Nobody can fix this but You, God. I'm giving this to You. I need Your help and Your answers."

The wonderful truth of God's Word is that God invites us to be His partners in a creative process that involves moving through our pain and to grow and gain what we can from it. There are lessons to be learned as you face and overcome your current pain and time of trouble. There's a path ahead that leads to a life of even greater purpose and deeper satisfaction. It most likely will lead to gratitude as well. I dare say you and I will probably look back and whisper, "Thank You, Lord." Not that you want to go through those life events ever again or have some warped mentality as a martyr for pain, but you know what the trial produced in you as you allowed God to work in you and on you; and for that...you are grateful.

Don't waste your trouble, trial, or pain! Don't sit down in it and hope it will pass.

Face it. Go to God with it. And prepare your heart and mind to learn from your pain, move through it, and move up: be propelled into a future that is brighter than anything in your past.

MOVING ON

What do you know you need to confront in
your life right now?

MOVING UP

What do you believe God will do with anything
you give to Him?

3

Taking Courage in the Crisis Moment

Eleanor was embarrassed that she had fainted. But the good news was that she hadn't fainted before she had lifted the fallen book-shelf off her young grandson—a feat that required almost super-natural strength—then resuscitated him using CPR techniques she had learned only two weeks before, called 9-1-1, talked sooth-ingly to her grandson until the ambulance and her daughter had arrived, been assured that her grandson was all right, and called two of her neighbors to assure them that everything was okay at her house!

In a time of intense difficulty, Eleanor had done her immediate utmost to change the immediate circumstance. That's the goal of every person in a crisis moment. When the tragedy strikes, we *want* to reverse course and bring about whatever change is neces-sary to right the sinking ship, overcome the terrifying adversary, or escape the deadly tragedy.

A wise man once said to me: "The difference between problems and crises is not necessarily in their size or the degree of upheaval they cause. The difference is this: Problems are slow. Crises are sudden."

I couldn't agree more.

A crisis is like a T-intersection in your life. It is a place of choice, with a decision that must be made. In a crisis, you will either turn toward what is good and godly, or turn toward what is negative and ungodly. You may sit at the stop sign for a while, but eventually you need to make a decision. The greater the crisis, the greater the urgency to decide.

A crisis may come upon us suddenly, as in the case of rapidly rising floodwaters or a 7.0 earthquake. Or a situation may build slowly over time until it is suddenly at the crisis point—the funds may have been depleting for months but now the account is empty; the arguments may have been escalating for years but now your spouse has walked out. There's no maintaining the status quo once you reach the crisis point. This is the time when action is required.

THREE PREDICTIONS ABOUT YOUR CRISIS

I can predict with great certainty that three things will happen to you when you encounter a crisis.

1. Exaggerated Emotions

When crisis occurs, emotions tend to become exaggerated. You may experience these three things in greater-than-usual intensity:

- *Blame.* You may be completely innocent when it comes to the reasons for the crisis, but that won't keep others from blaming you for the crisis and doing so with great vehemence.
- *Vacillations.* Those who react negatively in a crisis time can show vast extremes of temperament. They can be overly protective and smothering in their kindness one minute, and utterly rejecting and angry the next.
- *Combat.* Those who react negatively in crises very often turn on the people closest to them, seeking somebody to be the

focal point for their frustration and anger. People tend to lash out without even meaning to do so. The reality is, "close people" are usually the "safest people." Therefore, we tend to hurt those persons who we love the most.

Be on the alert for these tendencies in your own life. Refuse to play the blame game. Do your best to remain calm and steady and not emotionally reactive.

Refuse to play the blame game.

---

2. Revealed Motives and Loyalties

In a time of crisis you will discover who your true friends really are. A crisis separates your critics from your companions. When King Saul turned against David, only Saul's son, Jonathan, stood by David in loyalty. Everybody else in the court seemed intent on helping Saul track down David and kill him. Up to the time Saul turned against David, however, David was the darling of the palace. He was one of three people who joined King Saul nightly at the king's table for dinner.

Do not assume that all those who seem to be in your favor and loyal to you will still be loyal should the tides of popularity or prosperity turn in your life. Do not be surprised when even those you thought were close friends do not know how to handle your turmoil or minister to you in your pain. Recognize this as part of the process.

I have had the opportunity to see how people in ministry treat other ministers who suddenly face difficult personal situations, or are accused of things they may or may not have done. There is just as much tendency in ministry to distance oneself from problems as there is among non-clergy. People from all walks of life seem to think that if they associate with someone who is going through a problem, part of the stain of that problem will taint their own reputation. I've learned to not be surprised when this happens. Your closest allies are probably going to be people who genuinely do not think they have anything to either gain or lose by being your friend — they chose to be your friend because of who they are in character, who God is and what He calls them to do, and who you are in good times and bad.

I know I can rely on my friends who have the genuine character qualities that withstand crises.

I know I can rely on those who genuinely feel called of God to be my friends.

I know I can count on those who have known me and have experienced my loyalty through their own difficult hours.

The same is likely to be true for you.

3. Flee or Fight Responses

A crisis will bring about an instinct to either flee or stand up and fight. Our response is usually fast, spontaneous, and, at times, retaliatory. King Saul reacted to David's soothing music with a burst of jealousy and the throwing of a javelin intended to pin David to the opposite wall. King Saul's reaction was the exact opposite of a measured, reasonable, rational response! David had to act. If he hadn't, he would have died.

A crisis will bring about an instinct to either flee or stand up and fight.

If you are dealing in a crisis with someone who is mentally ill or who is reacting out of psychological compulsions, don't hesitate to act. You need to remove yourself as quickly as possible from their presence.

Some people are prone to psychological compulsions. They have irresistible impulses to perform irrational acts. Their compulsions rise from an intense inner pressure to have a need met. In Saul's case, he had a compulsion to be number one and he acted in totally irresponsible ways to ensure that nobody take his place in popularity among the people. When David was lauded for having killed ten thousand soldiers, and Saul was lauded for only having killed a thousand, Saul developed a compulsion to destroy David as an archenemy. There was no reason, no rationality in this. In truth, David was killing his ten thousand in *support* of Saul.

I have witnessed these same types of compulsions occurring in relationships in which one spouse or close associate becomes intensely jealous of the success enjoyed by the other. When one person takes more of the headlines, gains greater fame, and seems to be earning more success, the other close associate can become intensely jealous. In truth, the achieving spouse or associate is acting in good faith to bring greater acclaim to the entire family or partnership, and may even be acting in a way to bring greater opportunity to both parties in the marriage, business, or friendship. The compulsion seems to escalate, nonetheless, into very hot rage or very cold rejection.

The jealous person may demand more and more time and attention, hoping to curtail outside demands and notoriety, or the jealous person may push the achieving one away, claiming a need for space and greater opportunities for self. Sometimes both of these are in play almost simultaneously, to the point that the achieving person feels as if he is on a roller coaster. In the end, such a compulsion gone amuck can bring a disastrous crash to the relationship. And all along the way, there is nothing the achieving person can do—whether he fails to achieve or continues to achieve, he is criticized and pushed away.

In such a case there is no merit in delaying action. Part ways in peace and pray that the compulsive person seeks help and is healed. Please note that I am not recommending divorce or burning a bridge. I am saying, "Part ways." Give your relationship some distance so you can have greater objectivity in safety and possible restoration.

There was nothing David could do in the face of Saul's compulsive reactions except to duck and run. That is exactly what he did.

We live in a society that believes to "duck and run" is a cowardly act. In truth, it may be a very courageous act and it may very well be God's prescribed solution. I am not advocating abandonment but placing healthy boundaries on unacceptable and destructive behavior.

God did not tell David to pick up the thrown javelin and throw it back.

God did not authorize David to launch a political coup against King Saul.

The very opposite was true.

God led David to escape from King Saul's court; and for the next decade, at least, God provided for David as he went from place to place and had a wide variety of experiences—all of which solidified David's faith, produced some of David's most creative and famous psalms, and prepared David for his eventual leadership as king. When the time came for David to be raised up into the acknowledged position of king, he was ready, inside and out, to assume that leadership mantle.

You may find that God is leading you to "duck and run," at least temporarily. Very often that is exactly the prescription for situations involving abuse. Recognize, however, that even as you are moving away from the circumstances that seem intent upon your destruction, God is seeking to prepare you for even greater strength, and an even more effective life in the months and years ahead.

Walking away does not mean walking away from your purpose—it only means walking away from a particular situation or circumstance. Walking away does not mean you allow yourself to be diverted from what you know God has designed you to do. Never allow another person or situation to rob you of your destiny.

Walking away does not mean walking away from your purpose — it only means walking away from a particular situation or circumstance.

The temptation that may come to you in a crisis may not be a temptation to do evil. Rather, it may be a temptation to stop doing something good that you have been doing or that you know you are to do. I have often said, "If the enemy of your soul cannot get you in your weakness, he will try to get you in your strength."

The temptation may be to throttle back on your enthusiasm or to give greater credence to what other people think. The temptation may be couched in terms of "take greater caution" or "be less bold"—to the detriment of any forward motion in your life.

A crisis can cause a person to second-guess their decisions or to overevaluate their choices so that they choose nothing rather than risk making a bad choice.

Be aware of these tendencies and temptations and take them before God. Ask Him:

- From what should I walk away?
- How should I continue to walk?

COURAGE AS YOU WAIT FOR GOD'S LEADING

We often say we are willing to wait for God's leading, but then in a matter of hours, we begin to ask, "Why hasn't God acted?" God's timing is not our timing. He is never late…but He is also never too early.

Certainly God can change your circumstances in an instant. He can cause someone to come into your life overnight, open up a job for you in a matter of hours, or send you an abundance of resources within days. But it will be up to you to build that new relationship, work hard and keep that new job, or learn how to manage wisely that abundance of resources.

Also, be very careful in giving God the credit for changing circumstances in an instant. It may not at all be God who is at work!

Not long ago I heard about a man who had made a decision to divorce his wife, and the very next day, he met another woman. He thought this woman was the answer to all his dreams. She seemed to be the opposite of the woman who had cheated on him, manipulated him, and lied to him. He thanked God for sending him such a wonderful woman. He fell hard for this second woman and within a few months had married her.

To nobody's surprise but his, this second woman turned out to be an even worse manipulator, liar, and cheater than his first wife. This man had told her within hours of their meeting how miserable he had been with his first wife and why. She had learned very quickly what this man didn't like and had pretended to be the exact opposite person in order to trap him into being her husband. In truth, she had even greater problems and was even more deceitful than the first wife.

True, this man's circumstances had changed…but to say that it was God who had changed his circumstances is stretching the truth. In the end, this man had not changed. He had not allowed himself to be processed by God so that he truly could discern an honest woman from a deceitful one falsely marketing herself.

It takes genuine courage to hold a steady course and maintain faithfulness when it seems as if God isn't speaking or acting as we hope He will. God is always at work, turning all things to our good. But God's work is not always evident to us. We must not move to take matters into our own hands. We must have the courage to hold ourselves in check until God says, "Act now."

God is always at work, turning all things to our good.
But God's work is not always evident to us.

REINFORCE YOUR SOURCES OF ENCOURAGEMENT

Every person is subject to a natural human tendency to spiral downward in the face of a challenge. The spiral has several stages: feeling overwhelmed by the challenge, feeling inadequate for the challenge, feeling disappointed in oneself, feeling discouraged at the prospect of failure, feeling depressed about being a failure, and feeling dismayed that you can do absolutely nothing to change yourself or conditions around you. Let's break this down:

Feeling Overwhelmed by the Challenge

Step back and take a long look at the challenge. Don't react to it; respond to it. Most challenges that appear overwhelmingly huge can be broken down into bite-size pieces. I often say, "How does a person eat an elephant? One bite at a time!" Get perspective on your challenge. In all likelihood, if the goal is worthy, it cannot be accomplished in a day. Give yourself time. Develop a timetable with intermediate goals and subgoals. Above all, refuse to back away from the challenge. Take action against one aspect of the overall challenge.

Feeling Inadequate for the Challenge

After years of watching and dealing with human beings from countless backgrounds and walks of life, I have come to a conclusion that virtually every person on this planet is more aware of his or her weaknesses than their strengths. Stop dwelling on what you *can't* do, *aren't* qualified to do, have *never* done, or *don't* think you can do. Look at your in-born God-given strengths and abilities. If you need more skills, get them. If you need more information, get it. If you need additional preliminary experience, find a way to fold that experience into your life. God does not give us challenges that are beyond His ability in us. If God has presented a challenge to you, He has also promised that He will be with you in that challenge. What could possibly be beyond the ability of our omnipotent, omniscient (all-wise), eternal God? Nothing.

If a challenge seems too big for you, begin to see it as a challenge that is not too big for God! He stands with you. His adequacy more than compensates for any of your inadequacies. Your only job is to let God do His job.

At times, God may send someone alongside you to help you in areas of your personal weakness, as He did for Moses. Moses argued with God that he was inadequate for the challenge of going to Pharaoh and demanding freedom for the Israelites. God finally said to Moses, "I will give you Aaron as your spokesman" (see Ex. 4:10–16). If the challenge before you is God's plan, then He will send someone to you—you won't have to go out and search for that person. God will orchestrate your assistance, just as He orchestrated assistance for Moses.

Feeling Disappointed in Oneself

Many times we feel that we are facing an impossible challenge or a very difficult decision because we have failed in the past. We think we have set ourselves up for the current crisis. That may or may not be the case. What is certain is this: as long as you hang your head and continue to criticize your past or current actions, you will not move forward to tackle the challenge ahead. You will wallow in your own self-pity. Take personal responsibility for what belongs to you and leave the rest alone!

Yes, you may have failed. But that doesn't make you a failure or predict failure in your future.

Yes, you may have fallen short of your own standards. But that doesn't mean your standards are wrong and that you can't continue to pursue them and believe for them to be fully manifested in your life in the future.

Yes, you may have sinned or erred. But that doesn't mean God can't or won't forgive you. It doesn't mean God will no longer use you. It doesn't mean you have an excuse for not forgiving yourself and others, or that you are justified in not moving forward. Don't ever allow another's opinion of you to stop the predeterminations God has already made for you. Philippians 1:6 declares to be confident in this one thing: The same God who started the good work in your life is the one who will finish further and execute it! You can bank on that!

The same God who started the good work in your life is the one who will finish further and execute it!

Feeling Discouraged at the Prospect of Failure

Some people look at a challenge and can already see themselves failing at it. They'd rather do nothing than do something and fall short of the goal. There's an old saying, "Shoot for the moon. If you miss, you'll still land among the stars."

In the last decade, I have met and ministered to a number of professional athletes and their families. I am often inspired by their discipline and habits. Most of them have developed a wonderful ability to visualize their success *in advance* of their performance.

For example, a basketball player may close his eyes and see himself making the basket or the free throw, or the professional golfer may close his eyes and visualize himself driving the ball more than three hundred yards in the center of the fairway or making the difficult shot out of a sand trap. Singers and other performers also find benefit in such visualization. They visualize far in advance a stage appearance—hitting the high note, remembering their lines, or performing a stunt flawlessly.

God gives us this ability to visualize success as a part of preparing us to be successful. What we see in our mind's eye sets up a mental pathway that has a subconscious impact on other physical functions. The more we visualize our success, the more likely we are to succeed when we are under the pressure of performance.

God gives you an internal photograph of what you can walk out in life.

The truth is, if you aren't visualizing your successful accomplishment of a challenge, you are visualizing your failure at it! You may not be aware that this is what you are doing, but a failure to visualize success is nonetheless a huge step toward pre-accepting failure.

Don't set yourself up mentally for a failure that God has not authorized for you. God authorizes us for success, for winning, for achieving, for accomplishing, for surviving and thriving. Don't short-circuit God's plans by refusing to embrace them with your whole heart, soul, and mind.

Feeling Depressed about Being a Failure

Those who anticipate future failure also tend to anticipate that they will develop such a pattern of failing that they will become a "failure" as a person.

It doesn't matter how many times you have failed or fallen short of your desired results previously. What matters is how many times you have picked yourself up after a failure, dusted yourself off, and tried again. How many times as a baby did you fall down before you learned to walk all the way across a room, or run down a hallway? How many times did you fall off your bicycle before you were able to maintain your balance all the way down the sidewalk to the end of your street?

In all actuality, nobody is a failure until that person quits trying. Perhaps you produced results that hurt you or others. Perhaps you did not meet the goal you set out to obtain. Perhaps you fell short of the desired results—but failure only occurs as a result of giving up. Don't ever quit, but rather "fail your way to success by learning from your results."

The sad fact is that if you call yourself a failure, you will fail.

Not only that, but if you call yourself a failure, others will also begin to call you a failure.

What you say to yourself, and to others, about yourself determines to a great extent your willingness and ability to succeed.

Recognize that if God has put a challenge before you and promised to be with you, then God sees you as being both capable and worthy of being a success. He calls you to succeed. He sees you as His very successful, beloved child. Choose to see yourself as God sees you.

Choose to see yourself as God sees you.

Feeling Dismayed That You Can Do Absolutely Nothing to Change Yourself or Conditions around You

God spoke directly to Joshua, and to others, to not be "dismayed" (Josh. 1:9). To be dismayed is to be completely drained of courage and filled with alarm, apprehension, or anxiety. If that feeling of being dismayed escalates, a person can become paralyzed by fear. A person can become so depressed he will fall into despair, which often leads to suicide, isolation, or a complete withdrawal from society.

CATCH YOURSELF EARLY AND STAY STRONG

Don't allow yourself to ever become dismayed. You must continue to do those things that feed your faith. Catch yourself early in this potentially deadly downward spiral and do those things that provide ongoing encouragement to your soul and spirit.

Speak God's Word, and especially God's promises, aloud to yourself.

Memorize key verses from God's Word and recite them often.

Stay in fellowship with other believers who can encourage you, pray for and with you, and believe with you as you undertake the challenge before you.

Spend time with close friends who really know you and love you, and who will speak truth to you about the greatness of God and about the good things God has built into your life, including your inborn talents, your developed skills, and your experiences.

Listen to music and tapes that inspire you and remind you of God's faithfulness, dependability, reliability, and unconditional love.

Above all, keep the eyes of your heart and spirit focused on God, not the problem. If you keep your eyes focused only on your problem or challenge, it will loom larger and larger and eventually obliterate your vision of God. If you keep your eyes focused on God, however, He will loom larger and larger, and eventually will obliterate any fear you have regarding the situation before you.

The question is not, "How big is your challenge?"

The important question is always, "How big do you see God?"

The question is not, "How big is your challenge?"
The important question is always,
"How big do you see God?"

MOVING ON

How did you make it through the last major crisis
in your life?

MOVING UP

What would you do differently—with anticipation
of more positive results—if you were hit with that
same crisis again?

4

Look for the "New and Wonderful" in Your Life

The fire took everything Yolanda had loved. Her two young children, asleep in their beds, had died from smoke inhalation before the babysitter could get upstairs to them. Yolanda and her husband were called home from a celebratory dinner date they had planned for months to find their home in ashes and an ambulance carrying away the bodies of their five-year-old, Josefina, and two-year-old, Pablo.

On the night of the fire, Yolanda, in a daze and hardly able to say her own name, had been taken by firefighters and neighbors to a homeless shelter. Her husband, unable emotionally to handle the overwhelming tide of grief he felt, had driven away into the night. He did not reappear in Yolanda's life for several months, and then only to ask for a divorce.

Yolanda's family, hundreds of miles away in Costa Rica, encouraged her to return to the land of her birth, but they had no money to help her make the trip and Yolanda was reluctant to move.

As renters, Yolanda and her husband had taken out no insurance policy to cover their personal possessions so she had no way of recouping her material loss. Even so, she did not want to leave the United States. She had worked several years to attain citizenship, and she wanted to remain in the United States to build the life there that she had dreamed about for many years.

One afternoon in the homeless shelter, Yolanda was visited by a woman who offered her a home, part-time work, and friendship. She eagerly accepted the invitation and was grateful for a safe haven in which to regain some semblance of routine and emotional stability. One day her benefactor said, "Yolanda, God is creating something new and wonderful in you."

Yolanda said in a daze, "He is?"

"Oh yes. He is preparing you for something. I can feel it."

The idea was a totally new one to Yolanda. "New and wonderful." She kept repeating those three words to herself, sometimes voicing them aloud a dozen times or more in a day.

At first, Yolanda looked for the new and wonderful to appear *around* her. She was looking for a change in circumstances. Her present circumstances were acceptable, even comfortable. But she saw little that was "new" and couldn't imagine what might be "wonderful."

Then, she remembered that her friend had said God was going to do something new and wonderful *in* her. The more she explored that possibility, the more excited and hopeful she became. She asked her friend what she thought this new and wonderful thing might be and her friend replied very simply, "I don't know what it might be, but I know this — it will come from God."

"From God?"

"Yes, He is your Creator, and He is still creating you."

"I know He is the Creator of the world in the beginning," Yolanda said. "But I never thought about His creating me personally."

"Oh yes," her friend said. "God's Word says He created you from the foundation of the world. He is still molding and shaping you into the person He initially designed you to be."

This one brief conversation led Yolanda to break the bondage of living in the past and explore her personal possibilities, talents, giftings, and abilities. She decided to finish her high school education and earned a GED. She went on to take junior college classes in business. She recognized that she had always loved to sew, and she began to work in the evenings as a seamstress doing alterations, and later, she began to sew some of her own designs and sell them. Eventually, she hired two other homeless women to help her with what was becoming a rapidly growing business.

Yolanda also began to explore her spiritual gifts. She started attending church more regularly and going to Bible studies. She recognized that she had a gift for helping others, and she sought ways to put that gift into practice. With her friend, she eventually opened a special home for women who had been displaced by life's tragedies just as she had been. She personally worked to help each woman discover her own unique abilities and to find a job that might develop those abilities. And, of course, she sewed all of the curtains, slipcovers, and pillows for the home's décor.

While there will never be a replacement for her children, Yolanda did have a new sense of hope that arose with the realization she could and would spend eternity with them in the presence of God.

The process was not fast. All of this happened over an eight-year period. But in the end, Yolanda emerged a far more vibrant, focused, and fulfilled woman. And yes, she met a man five years after her great tragedy. They became acquainted at a church picnic, and today—ten years after Yolanda lost "everything"—she has twin sons, a happy marriage, a home, a business, and a ministry. Her favorite verse in God's Word is this: "And we know that all things work together for good to them that love God, to them who are the called according to his purpose" (Rom. 8:28).

Does every person who experiences the tremendous losses that Yolanda experienced emerge with such a glowing result? No. But the foremost reason is very likely this: not every woman who experiences tremendous loss is willing to do the difficult work of self-discovery and development, and to put in the hours of study and effort, to pursue the new and wonderful thing God has in mind for her!

New and wonderful.

New and wonderful.

New and wonderful.

Let these words sink into *your* spirit. What God had for Yolanda, He also has for you.

GOD IS STILL CREATING YOU

Creativity is a process. It is resident in God's nature and because God is both everlasting and utterly timely—He is omnipresent, in the now moment and forever—creativity is also everlasting and current. You are still a work in progress. Even now!

In truth, everything in life is process. There are some processes that simply cannot be shortened or bypassed if we truly are going to be all God has created us to be. Going through the prescribed process is what prepares us for what lies ahead.

- At times, trials and troubles are part of the process.
- At times, learning certain information or acquiring certain skills are part of the process.

- At times, the process erupts in joy or feelings of accomplishment or attainment.
- At *all* times, the process is intended for our growth, our refinement, and ultimately, our full creation as human beings. (In other words, moving on and up!)

When God first reveals Himself to us, it is not as a loving God, a merciful God, or a just God. He first reveals Himself as the Creator. He shows us His power, ability, and desire to create something out of nothing. God has never stopped creating. Every day is a new day of never-before-created mercies and miracles. Every baby born is a creation unlike any person born in the history of the world. Every person who experiences a spiritual rebirth is a new creation. Every person has a built-in capacity for creating, all of which occurs in the ongoing creative flow of God.

Every day is a new day of never-before-created mercies and miracles.

You are not like any person on this earth, or any person who has ever lived or ever will live on this earth. Your fingerprints, handprints, footprints, voice print, iris pattern, DNA, and all other facets of your personhood are one of a kind. In the same way, God's processes are unique to each person. The processes He has for *your* life are exclusively designed to help *you* become the person He initially planned from the moment of your conception.

No matter what any other person has ever said to you, let me assure you on the basis of God's Word that you are *not* an accident. You were planned and formed and fashioned before you were in your mother's womb by the hand of God in eternity (Jer. 1:5).

Let me assure you that you are *not* an unwanted child. You were wanted on this earth by God, your heavenly Father.

You are *not* without purpose. You were created with gifts that God intended for you to develop and use for your fulfillment and joy, and as a blessing to others to help them reach their fulfillment and joy.

And also let me assure you that, in spite of what circumstances may seem to say or what others may have told you, God *is* at work in your life, bringing you to the fulfillment of the person He says you can and will be. And let me affirm to you the glorious future God has for you.

GOD IS IN CHARGE

God created your ending, then planted you in your beginning. Your current reality is an episode in the ongoing reshaping of your life toward an established end. It is God who is in charge of your fashioning, and it is God who will create you until He comes to regard all aspects of you as good. God continually invites us to share in His creative process and to be His co-laborers in shaping our lives to line up with the destinies He designed for us even before we were born.

What good news this is!

You do *not* need to repeat past mistakes. You do *not* need to continue in the habits—physical, mental, or emotional—you have developed over the years. You can make the adjustments to position yourself in alignment with the good God designed for you. You can grow and develop new abilities to relate to other people. You can gain the information and insights necessary to avoid mistakes.

One of my favorite verses in God's Word is this statement God gave to us through the prophet Jeremiah: "I know the thoughts that I think toward you, saith the LORD, thoughts of peace, and not of evil, to give you an expected end" (Jer. 29:11). God's plan is for your good, and it is a plan that God expects to enact fully. What God expects does happen!

What God expects does happen!

I like the way *The Message* expresses this verse: "I know what I'm doing. I have it all planned out—plans to take care of you, not abandon you, plans to give you the future you hope for." Still another version of the Bible says: "'For I know the plans I have for you,' declares the LORD, 'plans to prosper you and not to harm you, plans to give you hope and a future. Then you will call upon me and come and pray to me, and I will listen to you'" (NIV).

Never forget these three central truths about your life and God's plan:

1. God knows you better than you know yourself.
2. God has planned for you things that you haven't even thought to imagine yet.
3. A plan is a design intended for fabrication. Plans are meant to be implemented. They are a predictor of precisely what is expected to come to pass.

GOD SEES YOU IN YOUR FULLNESS

One of the interesting aspects of God's creation is that God knows the fullness of our potential before He builds into us our gifts, abilities, and talents, and before He provides for us the opportunities to develop our potential. Let me give you two examples of this.

First, God sent an angel to speak to a man who was threshing wheat by a winepress. The angel said to this man named Gideon, "The LORD *is* with you, you mighty man of valor!" (Judg. 6:12 NKJV).

Nothing about Gideon's behavior, demeanor, or background would have led a person to describe him that way. Man of valor? Gideon's knees were no doubt shaking before and after this encounter with an angel. He was hiding out by a winepress threshing a little wheat in an attempt to hide his harvest from an invading enemy. Gideon himself was quick to argue that it didn't appear to him as if the Lord had been with him or his people. The angel replied, "Go in this thy might, and thou shalt save Israel from the hand of the Midianites: have not I sent thee?" In might? In strength? Gideon quickly argued, "My family is poor...and I am the least in my father's house." The angel said yet again, "Surely I will be with thee, and thou shalt smite the Midianites as one man" (vv. 14–16).

Gideon saw himself as an impoverished man under the siege of a fierce enemy. God saw Gideon as a judge of Israel and a mighty warrior who would deliver his people from the enemy that had a stranglehold on his land. Gideon *became* what God had already created him to be.

Second, God called David a man after His own heart long before David was a man! Nothing about a young lad named David seemed to be suitable for the role of king. He wasn't a relative of the current king, Saul. He wasn't of noble stature or the firstborn of his father's sons. To the contrary, David was the youngest of his father's sons, born to a sheep-raising family in a lowly town called Bethlehem. David was out in a back pasture tending sheep when the prophet Samuel came to his house, and nobody thought to summon him to the special feast that was prepared in Samuel's honor. Even so, before that day was over, it was David who was anointed by Samuel for eventual leadership of the Hebrew people. God called David "king" more than a decade before anyone else did.

Not only does God know the ending from our beginning, but He calls the persons He has made, us, "good."

At the end of each day of creation, as described in the opening chapter of the Bible, God looked at what He had created and said, "It is good." At the time of your creation—even before your conception—God saw who He had made you to be and He said what He said about all other aspects of His work: "It is good!"

God says this about you because of what He did in making you, not for what you have done since your birth. He continues to say, "It is good" because His plans and purposes do not change—nothing you have done and nothing that has happened to you has caused God to change His initial design and plan for your life. The you He made you to be is still the you He recognizes as the valid, authentic you...and the you He created you to be is still the you He desires to bring into the fullness of a radiant reality!

Nothing you have done and nothing that has happened to you has caused God to change His initial design and plan for your life.

Don't allow any person, thing, or event in your life to rob you of this truth. The core of you is valuable, worthy, and unchangeable. You cannot be defined by an act, incident, event, fault, opinion, or season of your life. The "real you," your authentic self, is who God says you are.

God calls things that aren't yet a reality as if they are not only real, but fully developed and accomplished. From His perspective, they are! God said through the prophet Isaiah: "Declaring the end from the beginning, and from ancient times the things that are not yet done, saying, My counsel shall stand, and I will do all my pleasure" (Isa. 46:10).

Nothing can stop God from doing what He chooses to do—and the great news for us is that God has chosen a tremendous future for each one of us. He invites us to choose for ourselves what He has already chosen. He invites us to fulfill what He has already prepared and planned. He allows us to become who He already says we are.

God has a plan for your life, a good plan! He invites you to participate in and cooperate with that plan!

THREE GREAT CHARACTERISTICS OF GOD'S GOOD PLAN

God's Word tells us that God's plan for each person is:

1. Personal

God deals with us individually. He communicates with us in deeply personal ways. He knows us fully and desires to reveal Himself to us. His purposes for us are purposes only *we* can fulfill—no other person is designed to do what we have been created to do. God's processing of us involves methods and timing unique to our lives.

What a great and glorious God we worship! He regards each of us as His prized, beloved child. His eye is always on us and He never forsakes us. He invites us to experience all He has created for us, and to embrace fully all He has planted in us.

2. Complete

God isn't "winging it" as you grow up and develop, as you struggle and persevere. He already knows why He made you and He sees you in your fullness. He knows where you are today, and He knows how to fashion you to become all that He sees you being tomorrow and next year and throughout your lifetime. You are tethered to your future with a bond that cannot be broken. This reality of truth removes a lot of unnecessary pressure and anxiety we put on ourselves in life. Relax, and learn to flow with the perfect plan of God.

3. Care-Filled

God is not the least bit haphazard about anything. He deals in details. His plan for you has been carefully crafted and is care-filled. He continually acts for your good (see Rom. 8:28). Note the words used in the prophecy of Jeremiah: "take care of you," "not abandon you," "prosper you," "not harm you."

If we ever saw the full plan God has for us, we no doubt would be awestruck by what God believes we can be and do. His plans for us are magnificent. They are intended to inspire us, motivate us, and to give us "hope and a future."

If you are going through a period of trouble or personal pain, you may find yourself thinking what many people think: *My best days are behind me.* People often think such thoughts in times of transition because they don't know their future. When a person is in a painful or dissatisfied present, the fantasized past starts looking better and better.

From God's perspective, your best days are always still ahead. God's future for you is always better than the past you have experienced.

God's future for you is always better than the past you have experienced.

Note that phrase from the King James Version of Jeremiah's prophecy: "to give you an expected end." That phrase holds profound meaning. It literally means that God expects His plan to be fulfilled in your life. Let me assure you of this: what God expects *does* come to pass!

Your sin...

The sin of someone else against you...

Your failure to live up to your own expectations...

The abandonment or rejection you have experienced...

Your mistakes or failures...

Your pain...

Your doubts or fears...

None of these things changes the expected end toward which God is fashioning your life. These things may slow down the process. But they do not stop or alter God's ultimate plan. Delay does not mean denial.

One of the greatest gifts you can give yourself is the power of "yes": "Yes to Your ways, Lord, yes to Your will. My soul says, '*yes!*'" Stop resisting what has already been established as the will of God, even when you cannot comprehend different events with your logical mind. If it is part of your destiny, you cannot lose it. If it is not part of your destiny, you cannot keep it!

No human being has the power or authority to alter what infinite and all-powerful God declares as His plan! His purposes *will* ultimately be accomplished.

GOD FINISHES WHAT HE STARTS

Perhaps the best news related to God's principle of processing is this: God our Creator is also God our Finisher.

The apostle Paul wrote to the church he established at Philippi: "Being confident of this very thing, that he which hath begun a good work in you will perform it until the day of Jesus Christ" (Phil. 1:6).

God is not only the One who created us but the One who enables and empowers us to become the fullness of our own creation. We cannot do it on our own strength. We can try...but we will always fall short of the fullness of His design if we fail to seek God's help and embrace God's processes.

We will always fall short of the fullness of His design if we fail to seek God's help and embrace God's processes.

Your current life is your opportunity to join with God in His creative processing, so that He and you together might bridge what was and is, to what *will be*. Participate with God in the creative process in order to move on and move up.

When you begin to see your life in this way, exciting things— new and wonderful things—begin to happen!

MOVING ON

Do you see yourself as being a "good" creation of God?
Why or why not?

MOVING UP

What do you believe God might still desire to create in you
or through you?

5

Refuse to Trade in Process for Progress

Kayla was about to marry husband number four when she glibly said to her friend Trina, "Oh well, who's counting?"

Trina replied, "Some people say—"

"I know, I know," Kayla interrupted quickly. "But I am making progress."

"How do you figure that?" Trina asked genuinely.

"Stop to think about it," Kayla said. "Derrick was great looking, right?"

"Right," Trina agreed. Derrick was one of the most handsome men she had ever laid eyes upon.

"But he had no ability to keep a job, and he drove a beat-up old car," Kayla said. "Then J.T. came along and he had a great car, a job, and he was also good looking."

"But—"

"Okay, so he had a little problem with alcohol and drugs," Kayla admitted.

"A little problem?" Trina responded. "He was a full-blown addict, and part of his 'great job' was dealing!"

"True," Kayla said. "That's why I left him, remember? But then there was Lars and he seemed to have it all—he was sober, had a good job, a great car, and was good looking."

"And every girl in town knew it!" Trina said.

"Okay, okay. He had a problem with being faithful," Kayla said.

"But now I've found Todd and he's got it all. He is good looking, has been in the same job four years, drives a nice car, is even buying a house, and he doesn't use or abuse. We've been together six months and I've never seen him look at another woman besides me. Like I said, I'm making progress!"

Trina replied, "I hope so, Kayla." But inside, she couldn't help thinking, *She's just changing players again. The guys change, but Kayla hasn't changed a bit through all these marriages. She's the same giddy, boy-crazy person she was eight years ago at sixteen.*

Trina added, "Why don't you give it a few more months before you get married?"

Kayla said, "What's the reason? I don't want to be single. It's too hard. I want a husband!"

Trina kept her question to herself: *But do you really want to be a wife?*

The sad truth is that I have met dozens of people who are just like Kayla. They mark their growth and change by looking at the externals instead of what God is trying to do in their own lives. They run from their troubles and pain to the next "quick fix," rather than allow God to work on them so they truly will be able to discern what is best for their lives, and to wait patiently until the best is brought their way.

OUR RESPONSE TO TIMES OF TROUBLE AND TRANSITION

Again, the entire process of growth and fulfillment hinges on a critical factor: the way we choose to deal with life's troubles, trials, and times of transition.

I'm going to give you a shocking instruction: embrace your pain rather than seek to escape it. It is in embracing an area of discomfort that you embark on the true way of escape—to a higher and better and more meaningful life. That's very difficult to see when you are hurting. During times of trouble we often see only the walls closing in on us. We want the pain to be over...right now! We wail, we rail, or we avail ourselves of the key to the liquor cabinet or the offer of drugs. We turn to the first available person as our "out." We shop too much, we eat too much. We seek to run and hide, only to be discovered again. Sadly, in all of our attempts to escape the pain, we dig ourselves even deeper into potentially damaging situations.

Embrace your pain rather than seek to escape it.

The only true escape from pain and discomfort is to embrace it—to recognize that it can be part of God's process for your refinement and reestablishment at a *higher* level and to a *better* place than you have ever known, if you allow it to be. That is not to say that God sends painful things to you to be processed. All good gifts come from the Father above. However, I often say, "If it is not God-sent, it will be God-used." He does use all things for your good (Rom. 8:28).

Our stance before God must always be, "Do what *You* desire to do in my life, in whatever manner and method You desire—I yield to them. I trust You with all matters related to timing and consequences. I put myself into Your hands and say as fully as I am capable of saying, 'Your will be done in my life.'"

REFUSE TO TAKE A SHORTCUT

Submitting one's life fully to God's processing means saying no to the shortcut that will inevitably appear.

Everybody likes a shortcut. A friend once described the short-cut that she took on her way home from school. Rather than walk on the sidewalks and pay attention to all of the stop signs and traffic lights along the regular route home, she sometimes headed across a park, over a series of railroad tracks through parked rail-road cars on the side tracks, through an industrial park, over a fence, and across a field that was often filled with tumbleweeds and other thorny plants. She may have saved ten minutes, but it was a hard ten minutes!

There are shortcuts in life as a whole, but they also tend to be more hurtful in the long run. We may think they produce faster results or quicker rewards, but what shortcuts really do is bypass or curtail the process that both prepares us and positions us for our bigger and greater purpose in life.

What tempts people to short-circuit or take a shortcut through process? The temptation of immediate progress. People want what they want, and they want it *now*. But God calls us to a journey — a process that is far longer and has the potential for being far more rewarding and joyful than a mere few moments of pleasure at reaching a goal.

In nearly every area of life, a quest for immediate progress thwarts the longer-lasting benefits of process. Yield to God's pro-cessing and patiently trust it. His processing always yields prog-ress that is both appropriate and in perfect timing. Remember, the existence of a building in height and strength is determined by its foundation.

TENSION IS PART OF THE CREATIVE PROCESS

All things that lead us to a new and better place in our lives involve creative tension. It is part of God's process of taking us from where we are to where we are designed to be. We need to embrace this tension with joy, anticipation, and enthusiasm that the expected end will be for our greater wholeness and benefit.

All things that lead us to a new and better place in our lives involve creative tension.

Creative tension is involved in learning and growing. Children experience growing pains as their bones, muscles, tendons, and other tissues grow and are realigned within the body. In school, children can often be seen with furrowed brows as they work on their homework, assignments, or exams—there's a tension involved in taking in new information, processing it, and committing it to memory. Invite God to expand your mind, heart, and spirit.

Does the tension keep a child from wanting to grow or learn? Far from it! Children experience a tremendous joy in learning something new and in growing to a stature that enables them to do and experience more.

This place of creative tension in our spiritual lives is the place where faith does its greatest work. It is the place where you will find the greatest rewards and satisfaction related to your own development as a human being. In fact, it takes creative tension for faith to function. (We'll talk more about the aspect of tension in chapter 8.)

LEARN TO SEE YOUR LIFE FROM GOD'S PERSPECTIVE

Your life is like a piece of embroidery. Every stitch God takes is a stitch toward the working of the whole—everything you encounter is put to use, every decision is worked into the whole, every experience is incorporated into the overall purpose. God truly is working all things together to accomplish His design for your life. His design is for good. His working is for good. Every aspect of His fabrication process has a reason and purpose that is ultimately for good.

God's Word also says, "The thing that hath been, it is that which shall be; and that which is done is that which shall be done: and there is no new thing under the sun" (Eccles. 1:9).

People sometimes interpret this verse to mean that every idea has already been thought and every emotion already felt. To a certain extent this is true—human nature is human nature, regardless of technological advances or cultural differences through the eons of time. The greater meaning of this statement, however, lies in the truth that you are who you were created to be from eternity. God finished you before He ever started you.

You will die with the same set of gifts, talents, propensities, and personality that you had the day you were born. The natural "you," with your own DNA—who you are—does not change in the natural world. The spiritual "you" can be rebirthed and renewed, but the end result of that spiritual birthing and renewing process is so the real you can emerge fully. Your spiritual renewal enables you to fully develop and use your gifts, talents, propensities, and personality to contribute good to this world. God's plan for you is in effect—your spiritual birth and renewal allows you to fully embrace God's plan and pursue it with your highest and best commitment and ability.

When you experience spiritual rebirth and renewal, you do not get a new set of talents or gifts. Neither do you get a new personality. Aspects of your personality may be subjected to refinement, and your gifts may be subjected to new disciplines and challenges, but the basic you is still the basic you.

What changes is not God's love for you or His plan for you, but rather, His freedom to engage you fully in His creative processes. As a forgiven child in right relationship with Him, you are now capable of being molded and refined in a unique way so the fullness of God's plan can be enacted. You are no longer swimming upstream in rebellion against the current of God's plan. Rather, you are flowing *with* God in the current of His purposes. Remember, God is a spirit and He reveals Himself to your "spirit being."

PREPARED FOR WHAT HAS BEEN PREPARED

Take heart that God is preparing you for what He has already prepared for you! There is a next level already fashioned for you. As you allow yourself to undergo the fullness of God's processing, He is fashioning you so that you will be ready for the day when God supernaturally opens doors and allows you to occupy a new role or step onto a new platform. Your spirit knows that!

God is preparing you for what He has already prepared for you!

God does not give us impossible dreams or unattainable desires. He teaches, guides, and counsels us step-by-step through life so that as we face each new opportunity or challenge, we are ready to take the next step of faith in what God desires to be a steadily upward and forward path.

Your challenge right now is not to ask God why things around you are changing, in transition, falling apart, or in upheaval, but rather to ask, "What next? What am I to learn and produce from this?" There's a reason and purpose in your discomfort, struggle, or time of trial. Find it. Begin to see your difficult time in perspective and how He is using it to prepare you and conform you, His beloved child! Always remember, God does not send "bad things" but He certainly uses them. Let your trouble be your servant!

MOVING ON

What does God seem to be changing in you?

MOVING UP

What do you sense God might be preparing *for* you?
Are you ready to move up?

6

Resuming Forward Motion

Charlene was shocked to see her name in headlines. She simply had not said what she was reported as having said. She had not done what she was reported to have done. In fact, she wasn't the person being described in the article.

To her great surprise, there was another woman in her community with her exact name—first, middle, and last. This woman had embezzled money, then had slandered those who turned her in, and then had attempted to skip town only to be tracked down and arrested and jailed.

It took two months for Charlene to clear her name with her friends, even though the newspaper did an article about the mistaken identity.

A year later, it took her six more months to unravel the paper trail related to identity theft. The "bad Charlene" had also read the articles about the mistaken identity, and had decided to conduct transactions in the "good Charlene's" name.

"I didn't do anything wrong," Charlene lamented to a long-standing friend who had come to town for a visit. "But just try to convince people of that! Everybody assumes that if you protest too much and declare your innocence too loudly, you must be guilty of something."

Sad, but likely true.

In other cases, people have moral lapses or yield to temptation.

They make mistakes. They fall down. Oftentimes, totally innocent people are married to spouses who make mistakes or fail.
The question that comes to nearly every person at some point in
life becomes this: *After this hit, can I stand tall and resume forward
motion?* No doubt you've asked that in your times of trial.

GETTING BACK UP AFTER A FALL

Have you ever witnessed someone in a foot race lose balance and
fall, or watched a professional football player take a hit and fall
and then not move?

I have.

There's a terrible feeling that hits the pit of your stomach. Will
the person be able to get up? Will he be able to complete the race
or return to the game?

The same feelings are sometimes ours in a time of pain and
transition. We wonder if we will ever be able to stand tall again,
much less move forward in our lives.

The short answer to the question "Will I stand and resume forward motion?" is yes... eventually.

The long answer is, "If you are willing to do what God asks of
you, you will stand and move forward sooner and faster."

The story of Abraham in God's Word gives us three vital
requirements for forward motion in our lives.

1. Obedience Is Required for Advancement

The first requirement for forward motion is obedience to what
God requires. The apostle Paul said it well when he said, "I was
not disobedient unto the heavenly vision" (Acts 26:19).

In calling Abraham to move out and possess the land of Canaan,

God told Abraham that he was to get up from the place where he was dwelling, leave his extended family members, and go to a place he had never gone before but which God would show him.

Abraham did as God said—mostly. God had told Abraham very specifically to get out of "thy country" and also "from thy kindred, and from thy father's house" (Gen. 12:1). Abraham left the country in which he was dwelling, but he did not fully leave all of his "kindred" behind. He took his nephew Lot with him, perhaps out of a sense of obligation, perhaps because Lot begged to go.

As you enter God's processing of your life—and His transitioning of you from where you have been to where He desires for you to go—be aware that you will face a tendency to pull your past mistakes and failures into your future. That's what Abraham did. He took a portion of his past into his future, against God's command.

What were the consequences of this? Abraham and Lot apparently got along fine until it became apparent that Lot and Abraham had each acquired too many flocks, herds, and tents of people to dwell together on the same pasturelands. Strife developed between the two groups of relatives, and they eventually went their separate ways. Lot chose the territory to the east, and he went to live on the plain of Jordan in the area of Sodom and Gomorrah. Abraham dwelled in the land of Canaan to the west, and set up his headquarters in the city of Hebron.

When God rained a judgment of fire and brimstone upon Sodom and Gomorrah, Lot certainly suffered a terrible loss, including his wife and all of his possessions. He escaped with only his two daughters. Abraham no doubt suffered, as well, at seeing the fate of his nephew and countless people associated with Lot, people he had known and cared for in the years before they parted. Even more critical to the history of both families was the fact that Lot's heirs became the Ammonites and Moabites, tribes of people who opposed the Israelites for generations upon generations. What had started out as an amicable uncle-nephew relationship became a history of war and pillaging between two opposing groups of people. The descendants of Lot worshiped false gods, the greatest tragedy of all.

There are things about your past that are better left in the past. Do not take anything into your future that God does not directly authorize you to take. When God says, "Let go," leave it!

Do not take anything into your future that God does not directly authorize you to take.

Keep in mind always that God will never advance you beyond your last act of direct disobedience and your repentance of it. God does not honor or bless rebellion, or disobedience. It is only when we repent—turn away from our error, seek to go in the opposite direction toward what is commanded, and embrace God, that He advances us and takes us to the next level.

It was only after Abraham and Lot separated, which is what God had commanded years before, that God spoke to Abraham and promised him that his descendants would be as numerous as the "dust of the earth"—an amount that could not be numbered. It was only after the separation that God told Abraham to lift up his eyes and look northward, southward, eastward, and westward, and then to walk through the length and breadth of the land that he saw. God said, "I will give it unto thee" (see Gen. 13:14–18).

God had a place specifically designated for Abraham, but Abraham could not move into that place until he obeyed God fully.

God has given us commandments and principles in His Word for the protection, preservation, and full provision of our lives.

Those who disobey His commands may succeed partially, but they will never succeed fully. They may achieve a modicum of recognition, material wealth, family heirs, and career success. But they will never experience a fullness of purpose, feelings of fulfillment, and genuine joy. Those are aspects of the spirit, and God does not bless us spiritually apart from obedience to His Word.

God also gives each of us very specific commandments about what we are individually to do and be. These commandments are never in contrast or contradiction to God's general commandments and the principles of His Word. They are, however, commandments that are directly related to our uniqueness as a person and to the specific times and circumstances of our lives.

In His general commandments, God tells us how we are to relate to Him and how we are to relate to others. We are to put God first and foremost in our lives, have no other gods besides Him, find our purpose in His identity, and structure our time and possessions to honor Him at all times. We are to love God with all our heart, soul, and mind. We are to love our neighbors likewise, as we love ourselves.

God's Word gives very detailed instructions about how we are to relate to God and other people as we develop a character that is obedient to God and loving toward others. Those who keep God's commands find themselves advancing along with others who keep His commands—the general commands are not only for our individual good but also for our good as a society. Salvation is an individual confirmation, as well as a societal one.

In His specific commands, God does not release us in the least from obeying His general commandments. His specific commands are like a second layer of commandments, ones directly related to our advancement as individuals. They usually are commands related to the perfecting of our character and the success of our work. When we ask God very specific questions about His plan for our lives, we can trust God to tell us specifically where we are to go, what we are to do there, how we are to conduct ourselves and accomplish the tasks He has put before us, when to take specific actions, and with whom to associate.

2. Vision Is Required for Motivation

A second vital requirement for moving forward is this: gain a clear vision for what is possible and what God still has ahead for you. God called Abraham to get out of his tent and to look upward. He said, "Look now toward heaven, and tell the stars, if thou be able to number them: and he said unto him, So shall thy seed be" (Gen. 15:5).

Gain a clear vision for what is possible and what God still has ahead for you.

You cannot see the heavenly canopy of stars if you are huddled inside your old tent. Tents confine you. They have limitations that do not allow you to see beyond their barriers. God will not give you a full vision of your potential—or of the fullness of the reward He has prepared for you—as long as you remain sitting down in the darkness of doubts, disbelief, and discouragement pegged to your past.

The phrase that is used in the King James Version of the Bible is, "he [God] brought him [Abraham] forth abroad," and then God told him to look up into the heavenly night sky. This phrase means that God brought Abraham out and built an invisible wall behind him so he could not return to his old way of thinking. It means Abraham's life was irreversibly set in a forward direction from that moment on. There was to be no going back.

People often say, "Don't burn any bridges." The truth is, there are some bridges in your life that should be burned. There are some things you should never go back to. There are some situations you should never enter again.

In nearly all cases, a transition time in our lives includes a required change in our thinking. There are old ways of thinking that we should set aside and leave behind.

Own up to your own mental habits. Are you aware that you have mental habits? Habits are not only physical; they involve our attitudes and our believing. We can become so accustomed to thinking in a certain way that we never stop to reexamine our thought life. In most cases, people aren't even aware that they have mental or attitudinal habits.

How might you determine your own mental habits? One of the best ways is to evaluate your first response to a comment that you consider to be hurtful, humiliating, or hateful. For example, if you overhear someone say, "I don't like _____," and your name is in that blank, how do you feel? And how do you respond? Do you feel angry? Do you feel rejected? Do you feel worse about yourself? Do you conclude, "I'm unlikable"? Do you retaliate with your own message, "I don't like _____," putting the other person's name in the blank? Do you say to yourself, "I don't like myself either"?

Or do you think, *Oh, they just don't know me very well,* or *They haven't known me long enough to think otherwise,* or even *They have their own prejudices and I'll need to work around those*? Do you think, *The good news is that God likes me*? Do you think, *That's okay. You don't have to like me. I like me. My friends like me. And those are the opinions that matter more*?

Do you think less of yourself because of what another person says about you?

Do you think less of yourself because of what another person says about you?

Your response to a negative comment about yourself is likely a habitual response. It is a way that you have grown accustomed to thinking after years of hearing or believing that other people don't like you for some reason, and not always the same reason.

The most important reason for recognizing that you have mental and attitudinal habits is so you might subject them to a rational process of examination. We need to ask about all of our mental and attitudinal habits: "Does this way of thinking and believing line up with what God says about me?"

If it doesn't, change the way you think!

The moment you hear or think anything that you know to be contrary to what God's Word says, immediately replace that thought with the truth. One of the best things you can do is say aloud to yourself, "But that is not what God says about me. God says _____," and then fill in the blank with the truth of God's Word.

The world may say you are stupid...God says He has given you a measure of intelligence and the ability to develop godly wisdom.

The world may say you are weak...God says you are strong when you factor Him into your life.

The world may say you are insignificant...God says You were worth the death of His Son, Jesus Christ, so that you might have eternal life and live with Him in heaven forever.

The world may say your best days are over...God says your best days are ahead.

The world may say you have sinned or erred to the extent that God cannot use you any longer...God says His plan is unchangeable and that He will continue to bring you to the fullness of His purpose for your life.

Why are we wise to speak the truth aloud to ourselves? Because the two ears that are going to hear that truth are our own.

Speaking the truth aloud reinforces the truth to our own lives and taps into the wellspring of faith that lies at our spiritual core. God's Word tells us that faith rises up and becomes active when we hear the Word of God (see Rom. 10:17).

It is by our faith that we are able to grab hold of God's vision for us.

What truly captivates our minds so that we do not want to return to old ways of thinking and living?

It is the vision of our future that God uses to motivate us forward.

When I was in my early twenties, God gave me a vision for my life. It was a life-changing experience for me. In just a matter of minutes, I gained a very clear and sure understanding about what God desired for me, and about what He wanted me to do for the good of others. There is no need for me to tell you in specific detail what God showed me in that hour of my life. It was His vision for my life, just like God has a vision for your life. I have discovered through the years that when some people hear about another person's vision, they often expect God to speak to them in the same ways and to call them to the same purpose. That is not the way God works. God speaks to each of us individually about His plan for our lives. He speaks to us in ways we can hear Him, and He speaks a word to us that is uniquely for us. The vision God has for your life is just that—it is for *your life*. The way God imparts His vision to you is a way that you will be able to take it in and fully understand it.

The vision God has for your life is just that — it is for **your life**.

The importance of sharing my vision experience with you is this: to inspire you to believe that God will impart to you His plan and purpose for your future.

I also am 100 percent confident that God will not impart His vision to you unless you are willing to get out of your own comfort zone and stare up into the heavenly expanse of His presence and say, "God, I want what You want for me."

In Abraham's case, God had already told him that He was going to be his shield, or protector, and also give him a great reward (see Gen. 15:1). The greatest rewards a person could have in Abraham's day were land and heirs. God had already showed Abraham that he would possess land. Abraham questioned God about the possibility of heirs. Having an heir didn't look possible to Abraham, given his age and the age of his wife, Sarah.

Abraham asked God about his reward.

Have you asked God what He has planned as your reward?

Through the years, I have met many people who believe that it is inappropriate or ungodly to ask God, "What's in this for me? What do You have for my good? What are Your rewards for me?"

Why are we reluctant to ask these questions? Is it because we fear God doesn't have rewards for us? Are we afraid our faith will become self-serving? Do we feel unworthy, or has "religion" taught us it is inappropriate?

None of that is true. To the contrary! When we genuinely and sincerely ask God to reveal to us His rewards, He does so, and the rewards He shows us *always* include a way for us to bless other people in tremendous ways. When God shows us "what's in it for us" He also shows us dozens, hundreds, or millions of people around us, and the greater answer He gives is, "Here's what is in this for you . . . and everybody you touch." What God reveals to us as being for our good, will be for our good in overflow proportions so that what we receive becomes a fountain of good that extends to countless other people.

Don't be afraid to ask God for a glimpse of His rewards to you.

His highest and best blessings will be for your benefit and become the means for you to be the highest and best blessing to others.

When God showed Abraham what He had for Abraham in the way of heirs, God's Word tells us that Abraham "believed in the LORD; and he counted it to him for righteousness" (Gen. 15:6). Abraham moved into a position of being in total right-standing with God. He *believed* the vision given to him, and therefore was in the right position for the vision to come to pass.

Any vision God gives you must be received by you. You must believe it is God's vision and you must believe it is for you. If you don't believe, or if you dismiss God's vision with all sorts of justifications and excuses, you will not be in a position for the vision to become a reality.

3. Sacrificial Commitment Lays the Foundation for Your Future

The third thing that is required for our forward motion is a sacrificial commitment.

After God had shown Abraham the land he would possess, and gave him a promise about the heirs he would have, God called Abraham to a time of sacrifice.

Just as vision is not given as long as we are inside the dark tent of our limited past, so sacrifice cannot be made inside the old confines of our limited past. No sacrifice was ever going to be made by Abraham while Abraham sat in his tent. Throughout God's Word, we find altars being built in open-air spaces, often on the tops of mountains. Even the altars associated with the tabernacle and the temple later in Israel's history were altars that were positioned so that there was no ceiling between the altar and the sky above.

God commanded Abraham to kill very specific animals and birds and place them in a specific pattern. Then, as the sun went down, a smoking furnace and burning lamp appeared. This was a sign of God's presence. Later, as the Israelites wandered in the wilderness under Moses' leadership, they were also led by a pillar of smoke (a cloud) by day, and a pillar of fire by night. From the most ancient of times, God had revealed himself to His people in fire. This flaming, smoking torch passed through the sacrifice that Abraham had made. And as it did, the Lord gave Abraham a message about his immediate future and the future of his heirs for many generations. In the aftermath of that experience, God forged a "covenant" with Abraham—a promise that God vowed to fulfill without variance.

Each of us is also called to make a sacrifice to the Lord in the light of what God has revealed to us about His plan for our lives. Certainly I am not talking about killing birds and animals. I *am* talking about making our individual lives ongoing and living sacrifices to God. We are called by God to sacrifice our time, talents, abilities, dreams, desires, and efforts to Him.

We are called by God to sacrifice our time, talents, abilities, dreams, desires, and efforts to Him.

What does it mean to sacrifice? It means to give God our future with a commitment that we do not recall. The apostle Paul told the early Christians in Rome, "I beseech you therefore, brethren, by the mercies of God, that ye present your bodies a living sacrifice, holy, acceptable unto God, which is your reasonable service" (Rom. 12:1).

We sacrifice when we say to God, "Here I am—all of me, all that I have, and all that I will ever have or be. Use me. Fulfill Your plan for my life. Make me, mold me, fill me, and spend me in any way that You desire."

Making such a commitment means that we set ourselves apart from our own ambitions so that we are available for God's purposes. There's an old gospel song that says it well: "I'll go where You want me to go, dear Lord. . . . I'll say what You want me to say."

Our sacrificial commitment seals within us God's vision to us in a way that nothing else can or does. When we say, "I am willing," God replies, "I will it to be so." He seals our commitment within us and it becomes the central and driving force that propels us toward our future.

I have met countless people who declare to believe in God. Some even claim they have "given" their lives to God. A fairly small percentage of people, however, are willing to look me in the eye and declare before God, "I have surrendered my entire life and future to God for Him to do whatever He desires in me and through me. I am 100 percent committed to giving God all that I have and all that I am for the rest of my days."

Most people give God only a portion of themselves.

They give God a portion of what they earn or possess materially, often what they consider to be excess.

They give God a portion of their time, often an amount they think is convenient.

They give God a portion of their interest or attention, but often only if they are asking God for something they want.

If you are truly going to be processed for the fullness of what God has for you, you must be willing to make a sacrificial commitment of *all* of you.

You must be willing for God's powerful presence to walk among the pieces of your life and impart to you His strength, His plan, His purpose, and His covenant that assures you: His plan does not and will not change, His love will not waver, His commitment to you is eternal. It is in this place of total commitment that you find fulfillment, satisfaction, and real intimacy. Surrendering your entire life to God is one of the greatest joys you will ever experience. The apostle Paul declared, "For in Him we live and move and have our being" (Acts 17:28 NKJV). Abundant life is waiting on your yielding to God and truly making him Lord of all!

His plan does not and will not change, His love will not waver, His commitment to you is eternal.

MOVING ON

Can you articulate a God-given vision for your future?

MOVING UP

What will it still take for you to make a *total* sacrifice of your life to God?

7

How Much of Your Spiritual Mind Are You Using?

Kendra sat in the middle of a large pile of wrapping paper, bows, tape, tags, and gifts—some wrapped and others still unwrapped. "It's all about presents!" she said gleefully to her friend Samantha who had come to help her with last-minute Christmas decorating and wrapping.

"Well, not exactly," Samantha said.

"What do you mean?" Kendra said, oblivious to her friend's serious tone. "Of course it's all about the presents! I can hardly wait to see what Jim gives me this year. It better have plenty of sparkle."

"Whatever happened to 'Jesus is the reason for the season'?" Samantha said. "You know, the true purpose of celebration and giving on this great day."

Kendra stared at her blankly. "Oh, that," she finally said light-heartedly. "Well, the presents are definitely the *seasoning* in the season!"

Samantha wondered when and if Kendra had a serious spiritual thought.

Years ago a phrase common to the American culture proclaimed, "A mind is a terrible thing to waste." In truth, there's even greater importance in this statement: "It is a waste to fail to develop a spiritual mind." In this transition time, as you struggle to move on and up, a well-developed spiritual mind is essential.

WHAT DOES IT MEAN TO HAVE A SPIRITUAL MIND?

Genuine spiritual thoughts are the product of a spiritual mind. These are not thoughts about spiritual matters; they are thoughts that bear spiritual substance. The realm of faith and God's creative processing is first and foremost a spiritual process.

Truly, all things that are created are birthed first in the spirit realm, and later are seen in the natural realm. Stop to think about anything you consider to be a wonderful invention or innovative process. It began first in someone's mind as a brilliant idea—perhaps only a fragment of an idea.

This is true, for example, of all things that are genuinely helpful to mankind. Faith-based charitable organizations, hospitals, schools, churches, and countless other beneficial and helpful institutions and ministries are birthed first in the hearts and minds of benevolent, kind individuals. Once the vision is established there, good deeds, bricks, and mortar follow.

THE SPIRITUAL REALM HAS NO LIMITATIONS

Your physical being is limited by what can be perceived by your senses. Your "inner vision," however, has unlimited capacity. It is in your inner being that God can impart to you what might be, what will be, what can be, what should be. That's the realm of unlimited living!

God's Word tells us that there is a carnal mind, and to be "carnally minded" results in death. There is also a spiritual mind, and to be spiritually minded is "life and peace" (Rom. 8:6). The carnal mind is also called the "spirit of the world" or the "fleshly mind." The spirit of the world stands in opposition to God. The worldly person wants what she wants, when she wants it, and the way she wants it. The opinions of others and the commands of God do not factor in to the worldly person's desires.

The truly spiritual mind is a mind alive with a spirit of faith, which is in harmony with God. The spiritually minded person wants what God wants and is willing to do things in God's time and according to God's methods. The commands of God form the boundaries for what the spiritually minded person desires. A concern for others is always a factor.

The spiritually minded person wants what God wants and is willing to do things in God's time and according to God's methods.

There are two things that a spiritual mind is not.

1. It's Not Positive Thinking

First, to have a spiritual mind is not the same as being a positive thinker, although it produces positive results.

Much has been written and said about positive thinking. From God's perspective, however, positive thinking is not a function of looking at yourself in the mirror and repeating phrases such as "You are wonderful" or "Today is a great day" until you feel energized by those statements. Such pump-you-up tactics are short-lived. The words you hear may motivate and energize you in the moment, but the words are going to be just that—momentary—unless those words are linked directly to the Spirit of God and His eternal Word.

Positive-thinking messages that come from the outside in do not have truly transformative power. Positive-thinking messages that truly change and empower us are the messages that the Spirit of God speaks to us in our inner spiritual minds and hearts, revealing the truth of God to us. That's why we say they are "inspirational." It comes from a root of "in spirit." Those messages that we receive by faith and begin to apply to our life are the messages that not only motivate us but empower us. They work from the inside out.

A person might tell you repeatedly, "You are lovable." You might say to yourself repeatedly, "I am lovable." A person may even speak to you what the Word of God says: "God says you are lovable" or "You are lovable in God's eyes."

Those statements may encourage you for the moment or for a season. But the real truth of God's love comes only as *you* read and contemplate God's Word and hear the Spirit of God speak to your inner spiritual mind, "I love you." When that happens, you will truly know you are beloved! And that truth transcends, overcomes, and endures through all sorts of outward expressions of rejection, alienation, or estrangement.

There are countless ways in which the negative messages from the outside world can negate, tear down, and destroy any positive messages. The roar of the negative is very often deafening and defeating.

In sharp contrast is the Word of God—the Spirit of God speaking to us in our inner spiritual minds the truth of God embodied in God's Word. When God says, "I care," "I want you," "I love you," "I value you," "I long for you," or "I delight in you"—and we know that truth with certainty because God Himself has spoken that Word to us in a way that is meaningful, personal, and establishing—then His Word trumps every negative word we might hear. It fills every depleted, empty place with His life-giving presence and power.

The person who begins to live in divine possibilities for life as a result of God's speaking to the person's spiritual mind—is a person who says in the face of all negativity:

- "It doesn't really matter what you say, world...it matters what God says."
- "It doesn't matter how you value or affirm me...it matters what God says."
- "It doesn't matter if you come or go, ultimately...it matters only that God says He will never leave me nor forsake me. He will never reject me or throw me aside. I am His beloved and He is mine."

The person with a spiritual mind is a person who truly can be resilient and rebound in a positive way—not just some of the time, but consistently over time.

2. It's Not Pumped-Up or Mellowed-Out Emotions

The spiritual mind is not the product of pumped-up emotions. Neither is a spiritual mind synonymous with mellow emotions such as caring or compassion or sensitivity. Although many deep and significant emotions—such as joy, love, compassion, faithfulness, and mercy—are directly associated with spirituality, the presence of these emotions does not give a person a spiritual mind.

Rather, the person with a spiritual mind exhibits such emotions as the by-product of a relationship with God. The relationship comes first and leads to the emotions, rather than the emotions producing a relationship. You will only be transformed if you learn to draw life inspiration from God's Word and develop a relationship with God.

Begin to read God's Word daily as food for your spirit and trust the Spirit of God to teach you and to reveal to you who you are and how much God loves you. Get the truth of your worth from God, and your worth will be true in all circumstances and relationships. Let the truth of God's Word establish you and energize you. Let it empower and enrich you. Begin to communicate with God and become thoroughly familiar with His character. Nobody can do for you—and you cannot do for yourself—what the Spirit of God can do in your spiritual mind.

Nobody can do for you — and you cannot
do for yourself — what the Spirit of God can do
in your spiritual mind.

In sum, develop a relationship with God, and you will have an ongoing, abiding, constant source of encouragement and empowerment.

DEVELOPING A SPIRITUAL MIND

As a person takes in the Word of God daily, two things begin to happen simultaneously. First, the Word of God cleanses away carnal thinking and faulty mental habits. There is a "washing" of the mind that occurs as a supernatural work of God. I cannot fully explain this to you other than to say old patterns of thinking no longer are effective or satisfying. In my opinion, there is no true lasting behavior modification without the Spirit of God. All behavior stems from belief. A faulty belief system will produce faulty behavior. The Word of God is truth. Truth functioning in your life brings transformation. There is a growing desire for doing things God's way and for understanding deeper and deeper spiritual concepts. Old opinions that are "me first" in nature become distasteful and undesirable. Old concepts about how things work and why seem outdated and ineffective. There is a desire for a newness of life and a newness of thinking and believing.

Second, the Word of God instills in a person a new perspective. As you have insights into God's Word, you will find that you have an increased perception, which carries with it an increased capacity for comprehension. You begin to "see" things from God's perspective—including those things that are not presently an external reality but may very well be an internal reality or a reality that is about to burst from the spiritual realm into the physical and material realm. It is an internal photograph given to you by the Spirit of God. Those who have God's perspective see with spiritual eyes, and understand in the depths of their spirit, what God is doing in our world and in themselves, for the most part. They see reasons for things that seem unreasonable. They comprehend purpose for things that seem random. They are able to understand principles and concepts that underlie seemingly superfluous facts.

The spirit deep within a person is only fully taught and changed by the Spirit of God. Every other form of instruction or motivation is incomplete or lacking in some way.

PRACTICAL INSIGHTS INTO READING GOD'S WORD

There is no substitute for reading God's Word daily. Just as you wouldn't choose to go without food for your body, make a choice not to go through a day without food for your spirit. Spend some set time each day reading God's Word, in a translation or paraphrase that is both easy to understand and meaningful to you. If you have been reading God's Word for years, you may want to try a new translation or paraphrase that can trigger a new understanding of God's message.

There is no substitute for reading God's Word daily.

Sometimes you will find it very helpful to spend two or three sessions of reading in a day. The hungrier a person is for answers to her life's problems, the more she can benefit from reading her Bible several times a day, in short time periods so she really can take in what God's Word says.

Ask God as you begin to read to help you understand the meaning of the passage, and also ask God to help you see an application of the Scriptures to your life. After you have finished reading, ask God to seal what you have read to your heart and mind so that you can think about the passage in the coming hours of your day, or over the next days and weeks of your life.

Very often as you read your Bible, certain words or phrases will seem to have special meaning to you. Underline or highlight those words. Make notes in the margins of your Bible.

I also recommend that you keep a notebook or journal nearby when reading the Bible. Write out complete verses that stand out to you. You may want to commit these to memory, or have them available for reference and contemplation. Also, write down any insights you have into the meaning of a passage, especially insights into ways you might act on that passage in your relationships and as you undertake your daily, practical responsibilities. If you have questions, write those out so you can talk to God about them in prayer, and perhaps ask others who know the Bible well where you might find answers to your questions.

ALL THE ANSWERS YOU NEED

The Bible holds *all* the answers to life's deepest questions and needs. God does not expect you to go through life without guidance, answers, purpose, and understanding.

The challenge for many people is in finding the answers to specific concerns.

To get the right answers, of course, you need to ask the right questions. Go to the deepest emotional and spiritual level of a problem or issue. The Bible doesn't have a specific verse related to computer glitches, nor does it have a verse that applies to automobile problems. The Bibles *does* have many verses related to patience, wisdom, seeking help, taking advice, making choices, and trusting God to be the source of all answers and help that you need.

When seeking answers, go to God's Word with an open heart and ask, "What do You want to say to me today? How do You want me to change and grow? What do You want me to learn about You or about myself? What do You desire to affirm in me, or remove from me?" We go to God's Word to be fed by what we hear from God.

One of the greatest things I have done in my life is build a firm foundation of truth by habitual study of God's Word. I did not wait until there was a storm to build an ark. Noah was commanded in the book of Genesis to build an ark by faith and obedience to God before he ever knew what a storm cloud or lightning bolt looked like. By doing so, he was not only covered in the storm but also carried. I encourage you to build an ark, a shelter of safety, by faith, before you ever know what a "cloud" looks like. If, however, you're already in a storm — it's still a good time to build a boat!

READ WITH FAITH AND RECEIVE GREATER FAITH

Genuine revelation about how to live — and genuine encouragement and inspiration that empowers a person to live according to God's principles — comes as a person reads God's Word with faith.

What does it mean to read with faith? It means to read God's Word with the perspective that God has something for you. God desires to speak to you, change you, and transform you in some way by what you read in His Word. Very often a person will find it helpful to pray aloud before he or she begins to read the Bible, "God, help me to focus on what Your Word is saying to me about my life. Reveal to me the truth that You want me to live out today."

God desires to speak to you, change you, and transform you in some way by what you read in His Word.

To read with faith means to read with an *intention to believe.* It means a person approaches the Word of God looking for truth and believing that truth is about to be discovered.

To read with faith means to read with a *desire to apply.* It means a person approaches the Word of God intending to put into practice the concepts and principles found there. It means having an intention to obey what is commanded.

The wonderful thing about reading God's Word with faith is that a person's faith is made stronger and more powerful. A cycle is set in motion. Read with faith, have more faith, read with greater faith, develop even stronger faith.

Faith is the engine that drives a spiritual mind. It is the core of the life of unlimited possibilities. Faith is the built-in encouragement and inspiration that gives a person a surge of desire to obey God, as well as ongoing perseverance in obedience. Faith is what enables a person to turn spiritual thoughts into spiritual actions.

You cannot engineer faith or create it on your own. It comes to you as a gift of God as you read and hear God's Word. To hear means more than your ability to perceive through sound. It refers to your "taking in" God's Word in such a way that you remember it and it becomes a basis for your subsequent actions. A person can listen to all sorts of things, and hear very little. To truly hear is to listen with the intent of understanding, applying, learning, and allowing what you have heard to impact your thoughts, attitudes, feelings, and beliefs. This is done as you rely on and cooperate with the Holy Spirit.

There's a vital step that most people do not seem to take. A person must recognize that God desires us not only to read and believe but to *apply* what we have read and believed to the practical circumstances of our lives, including our conversations and actions toward all we encounter in any given day. The Word of

God is intended to change us from the inside out. As we change, things around us change.

"Living" the Scriptures involves far more than "learning" the Scriptures. It means that we read, we believe, and we apply. Then faith grows.

THREE THINGS FAITH ENABLES YOUR SPIRITUAL MIND TO DO

Faith activates the function of a spiritual mind. The carnal mind does not function with faith. The spiritual mind cannot function without it. Very specifically, there are three things your faith enables your spiritual mind to do:

1. See opportunities instead of opposition.
2. Make decisions based upon principle rather than preference.
3. Have greater sensitivity to *kairos* moments.

1. Opportunity or Opposition?

The spiritual mind embraces the opportunity that is resident in tension, rather than seeing tension as a form of opposition. This is very different, of course, from the way the natural mind functions. In our flesh, we do our utmost to relieve tension or pressure. We take pills to mask tension; we get a massage to relieve tension; we work out to release tension. We walk away from a tense situation or a conversation that has become more intense than we desire.

In our attempts to escape tension or pressure, we do not allow God to do His creative work. Faith calls us to embrace tension as part of the process of manifesting evidence and allow God to stretch us in ways that will produce a new and good result. Rather than walk away from the difficult course, we take the course, allowing our faith to function and depend on the Holy Spirit to provide His fruit (as found in Galatians 5:22–23 of love, joy, peace, longsuffering, gentleness, goodness, faith, meekness, and temperance). This is where and how we develop, learn, and transform. Rather than walk away from the difficult conversation, we engage in the conversation and grow from it. Rather than seek to escape the tension of the workload, we confront the workload and either conquer it or determine what must be managed in a different way.

Faith calls us to embrace tension as part of the process of manifesting evidence and allow God to stretch us in ways that will produce a new and good result.

In the spiritual realm, when we feel tension, the wise response is to act in faith, trusting that God is leading us to a new opportunity or a new level of maturity, which always inevitably includes exciting and expanded rewards, and a deeper relationship with God.

2. Principle or Preference?

The spiritually minded person chooses to live according to the principles of God's Word, rather than by human preferences.

Preferences are negotiable. They very often are matters of personality or style—which varies and is always subject to fads.

Convictions are not negotiable. They are based upon the fixed truths of God's Word.

God's Word tells us we are to walk by faith, not by sight—in other words, we are to live according to and in alignment with what God's Word says and not according to the way things appear in our immediate environment. We are to walk according to lasting, fixed, sure principles, not according to factors that change from place to place or from year to year. What is a "personal conviction" cannot be placed on others simply because you prefer it.

The character traits of God, of course, are among those fixed principles. God does not change His nature. He is always *I am.* He remains constant to what He says He is—always, in all situations, to all people. He is not a discriminator or "respecter" of any particular person.

Faith established on the fixed principles of God is faith that produces positive results. And faith is "an equal opportunity business."

3. *Kairos* or Chronology?

God's Word tells us that we are to walk in wisdom, "redeeming the time" (Col. 4:5). The word for "time" in this phrase is *kairos*, which is basically "God's timing." *Kairos* is a pivotal point at which something is destined to happen. It is the point at which eternity invades human history. It is the intersection between God's sovereignty and man's destiny.

Chronos time—which gives rise to our word *chronology*—is time that we set our clocks and watches by. It is a ticking of seconds to create minutes to create hours. The carnally minded person is concerned primarily with chronology. It is the time continuum for appointments and deadlines.

The spiritually minded person sees life events through the lens of eternity. She recognizes that God is working continually and constantly to enact His plans and purposes. In *kairos*, God is never too early or too late. Nothing happens by chance. All things happen when they are authorized and appointed by God to happen.

From the perspective of *kairos*, nothing happens instantly, even though we may think of certain things as being "instant" because they appear suddenly or we have a moment of awareness that something has changed. In truth, anything that appears to us "instantly" is something that has been in preparation from the foundation of the world!

God already knows your tomorrow. In fact, He not only "knows" it as an awareness but has finished and completed it before you ever enter it.

He has already prepared for you all things that you will need tomorrow.

He has already prepared for you all things that you will need tomorrow.

He has already provided for you in the spiritual realm all the resources that will be required for you as you step into your future.

The entire concept of time is primarily for the benefit of man. We human beings need for things to happen "over time" so that we can take them in. Every process is set in time, and this is for man's benefit. Most people do not respond positively to sudden shifts or changes. Time serves as something of an usher, guiding us forward toward those things God has prepared for us but which we have not yet received or experienced in a natural realm.

Time allows you to become prepared for what is already prepared for you.

The bottom line is this: You will find it extremely difficult to get through any time of trial, pain, or transition without a spiritual mind enlivened by faith. You cannot move on or up without it. Faith is the catalyst that turns change into renewal, and trouble into transformation.

MOVING ON

What is the state of your spiritual mind?

MOVING UP

What do you believe God might have for you to discover and learn as you dive deeper into His Word?

8

Develop the Faith That Overcomes Fear

Myra had been one of those who was running for her life on 9/11. A giant wall of dust and ash bellowed down the avenue behind her and threatened to overtake her and hundreds of others who frantically sought shelter as the first World Trade Center tower collapsed. Years later, she felt as if she were still running.

"I don't remember being afraid of very many things when I was a child or teenager," she confided to her friend Suzanne. "Now I can't think of too many things that don't make me anxious or afraid."

"Like what?" Suzanne asked, noticing that Myra's fingers were trembling even as she held a mug of hot cocoa with both hands.

"I'm afraid the subway train will stop in darkness and none of us will be able to get out of the cars or know which way to run. So, I take a bus and my commute to work is twice as long. I'm afraid my children are injured if they arrive home five minutes later than they say they will. I'm afraid my husband won't come back from a business trip—that his airplane will crash or his car will careen over a cliff."

Her tone was wistful and tears welled up in her eyes as she added, "I don't want to be afraid, but I am. I don't want to live this way. It seems my fears are growing stronger, not weaker. The world is a frightening place to me, and on most days I want to run and hide and take everybody I know with me."

Many people seem to live where Myra lives emotionally. Their fears may not be the result of surviving 9/11, but their fears are equally grounded in a dread of the unknown and a deep feeling of insecurity. Fear absolutely keeps you from moving up.

THE FOREMOST KEY TO OVERCOMING FEAR

Faith and doubt aren't opposites; faith and *fear* are opposites. It is faith that enables us to overcome fear. But even more specifically, it is faith that has graduated into trust that allows us to live with confidence. And it is trust that allows us to do more than move on, but to move up.

It is faith that enables us to overcome fear.

How do we develop faith that graduates into trust?

The simple, short, and profound answer is to accept God's love. It is when we feel fully assured that God loves us and out of His infinite love, He gives to us the fullness of His provision, protection, and presence, that we experience confidence and peace. This brand of peace is deep and abiding. It is a peace that is rooted not in what we perceive or "feel" but rather in what we know to be true about God and His love for us.

Where do we learn the truth of God and His love? In God's Word. The understanding that is required, however, is very specifically related to a knowledge of God's character.

Many years ago, I asked the Lord, "Who are You?" I knew some things about God at that time, but I wanted to know more.

I felt impressed to go to the Psalms, and as I read and studied them over a period of time, I wrote down every character attribute of God that I saw there. I tried to read the Psalms through the eyes of David, since he wrote many of them.

I discovered that God is:

- Patient
- Full of mercy
- Longsuffering
- Holy
- Loving
- Protecting
- Nurturing
- Caring
- And so much more!

I invite you to read the Psalms and make the discovery of God's character for yourself. There are literally dozens and dozens of character-trait attributes identified by the psalmists. All of these give insight into the nature of God, and our believing that these are the character traits of God expand our faith to receive more of God's love.

After you have explored the Psalms, begin to read the Gospels — Matthew, Mark, Luke, and John — with a heart open to discovering the character traits of Jesus. As you read through the miracles of healing and deliverance, write down the character traits you see at work. As you read what Jesus taught, write down the traits you believe are behind His words of instruction and encouragement. As you read the accounts of the crucifixion and resurrection, note the character traits Jesus displayed.

You very likely will find that the character traits of God the Father are the same as those of Jesus the Son. God's nature is constant through the ages. His character doesn't change from circumstance to circumstance, or from one person to another. God's character is always rooted in love. His actions are always motivated by love. His promises are guaranteed by His love. His forgiveness and mercy are extensions of love!

It is one thing to believe in an awesome, all-powerful, all-wise, all-creative God. Faith is believing that God is, and that God is good. Faith is rooted in believing that not only is God capable of acting on our behalf for our eternal benefit but He desires to do so.

Trust is believing that God cares and God loves. Trust is believing not only that God can but that God will. Why? Because God loves.

Trust is believing not only that God can but that God will.

There is a difference. Trust is what overcomes our deepest fears because, as the old hymn says, "I know *whom* I have believed."

As a mature adult functioning in a normal circumstance or relationship, you are not likely to trust a person you don't know. For example, you wouldn't normally leave your child in the care of a total stranger, or hand over the keys to your home to a stranger standing on the street corner. In a similar manner, you are not likely to trust God completely with every aspect of your life if you have never taken the time to get to know God.

LOVE ACTIVATES FAITH

Love is the precursor to faith, and faith activates everything in the spiritual realm. God's Word tells us that "God so loved" that "God gave" (see John 3:16). This powerful force of love is what undergirds your faith. When you know you are loved beyond measure, you are willing to apply your faith to the circumstances around you because you have a confidence that the God who loves you will never fail you.

You are willing to believe for something better in your life because you believe God loves you and desires something better for you.

You are willing to trust God to work a miracle on your behalf because you believe God loves you and wants you to experience His full provision for you.

You are willing to take a risk and embrace change because you believe God loves you and is at work creating the very best possible life for you.

The process goes like this: First, we learn about God's character from the Word of God. Over time, we find ourselves communicating with God, whom we love and who first loved us. The more we understand God's character, the more willing we are to open ourselves up to receiving His love—the more open we are to moving on and up. The more we receive His love, the more willing we are to pursue His promises and act on His commands.

The more we receive His love, the more willing we are
to pursue His promises and act on His commands.

Second, as we put our faith to the test, we discover that God is always completely faithful to His Word. In fact, He makes Himself one or synonymous with His Word (see John 1). He does not change. He does not reject us. He does not abandon us or forsake us. His Word will never fail us.

Our challenge, therefore, when it comes to developing confidence and fearlessness, is to read God's Word regularly and to communicate with God consistently, and at every opportunity, to apply God's Word to real-life circumstances and gain evidence for ourselves that God is who He has declared Himself to be. We must choose with our wills to obey the commands of God. He reveals Himself and gives His full blessing only to those who seek to obey Him and are not rebellious against Him.

TRUST THAT IS UNWAVERING

Trust becomes unwavering in us as we put God's character and promises to the test in our daily lives—in our periods of pain. Faith becomes trust as you experience the ways in which God answers prayer and works all things to your good as you love and obey Him, and you discover a steadfastness in your heart as you rely on God to be with you at all times and in all circumstances.

Faith, in general, is the persuasion of the mind that a statement or idea is true and worthy of trust. God's Word says it this way: "Faith is the substance of things hoped for, the evidence of things not seen" (Heb. 11:1). Faith is having a deep assurance or conviction that what you are hoping for—which is based upon what God's Word promises—will indeed come to pass even if you see no external evidence for it.

Faith functions as a force of illumination, allowing us to "see" into an area that is currently "unseen." A pregnant woman knows that the child within her is real, long before there is any evidence.

Before she feels the child moving, before she sees evidence of the child in her extended abdomen, she knows that her child is real and alive. She believes she will give birth. This is the very essence of faith. Long before we see, we believe. The world tells us to "see and then believe." God says, "Believe, and you will see."

The world tells us to "see and then believe."
God says, "Believe, and you will see."

Faith always exists in a context of unfulfilled longings and desires. We simply do not acknowledge our need for faith or use our faith unless there is something in our lives that we desire and do not have.

When we know God loves us too much to allow us to fail, we are willing to take the risk of believing in and trusting Him.

TRUST IS DEVELOPED THROUGH DIVINE MOMENTS

When we receive a divine moment—an intervention of God into our circumstances—and act, we grow our trust. We must be aware that we are in the midst of a divine moment so we can act on it. Divine moments never look ordinary. They are discerned by people with an active faith—they have a God quality to them. Divine moments exist in a dimension of eternity—a state of being that transcends human design. There is a sense of "fullness" to these moments, as if something that has been intended since the foundation of the universe is about to be revealed and to burst forth into revelation.

If you learn to see and discern divine moments, you can move quickly into them and take hold of all God has for you in that instant. If you fail to see the divine moment, you will let that moment slide by. Your trust in God will not grow. To avoid missing those moments, you must learn to shut down that noise of life. Most times when Jesus addressed people, He did so by saying, "He that hath an ear let him hear." He was not talking about the appendages on the sides of your face, but an "inner ear" within your spirit.

I heard not long ago about a woman who felt God had called her to be a missionary when she was eighteen. She was able to describe vividly the moment when she knew with certainty that she was to go to Russia with the gospel, and to go quickly. A missionary who had come to her church for a Sunday evening service announced that she was leaving the next week for Russia and was looking for a traveling companion and assistant. Everything within this young woman said, "Yes! This is for you! Go now!" The moment was hers—it was a pivotal point of destiny for her.

This was in the early 1960s and Russia was in the grip of communism as just one of many states in the Soviet Union. All evangelistic efforts were underground at that time. Most of the churches had been closed or turned into museums. This young woman reasoned that she needed more training, more time to prepare, better political conditions, a better knowledge of the Russian language, and so forth. She did not act on the divine moment.

And that moment never came again.

She traveled to the Soviet Union several years later but was not able to stay, or even to make good contacts with Christians there. In subsequent decades, she attempted to go to the Soviet Union to work and minister—but all doors closed. She never lost her desire to go or her love for the Russian people. But she lost her divine opportunity to go. She did other good things with her life, but she missed out on what would have been the fullness of her destiny on this earth.

The person with sensitivity to divine moments lives in the counsel of godliness, which means always looking for what God is doing, what God is saying, and what God is desiring (see Ps. 1:1). It is the person who is constantly looking for God's next directive who makes choices and decisions that truly produce lasting fruit, vitality, and fulfillment, and who grows in trust. Such a person remains steadfast in times of adversity. For those who learn to live with an awareness of divine moments, life unfolds as a continual series of blessings that take a person from strength to strength, and from glory to even greater glory. This is spiritual advancement.

On November 18, 1995, I was sitting in a church service watching a fairly bland little video, and I suddenly began to weep deeply. A man of God came to me and said, "This night God has removed every hindrance and every obstacle that has held back every harvest of God from your life." The next day, after years of struggle, we received an abundant breakthrough. And shortly thereafter, I circled the globe in a period of thirty days. I preached and prayed for hundreds of thousands of people, personally laying my hands on many people for the fire of God to activate their hearts for evangelism to reach the world. The worldwide ministry God trusted me with was launched and it has continued since that time.

Whatever you do when you enter that divine moment in your life sets up a future outpouring of blessing.

You cannot create a divine moment. You cannot create your own destiny. You can only discern a divine moment and enter into God's plan for your destiny.

If anybody ever asks you why we need faith, here's your answer: we need a spiritual mind alive with faith in order to live above fear and to walk in confidence; we need to make wise decisions

You cannot create a divine moment. You cannot create your own destiny. You can only discern a divine moment and enter into God's plan for your destiny.

based upon principle, receive divine moments, and live in ways that yield eternal benefit. The spiritually minded person seizes all godly opportunities, makes godly choices, and develops a perspective that encompasses eternity. The person with a lively faith never just moves on—she also moves up.

WALKING DAILY BY FAITH

A daily walk of faith—using our spiritual minds to live out God's Word—is not easy. Don't ever let anybody tell you it is. The reason it is difficult, however, is not a great mystery. The root of fear lies in what we don't know. I believe perhaps the greatest frustration and cause for anxiety stems from the fact that we do not have a clear view of what lies around the next bend. We don't know what the next hour holds, much less tomorrow or next week or next year.

It's this lack of knowing that creates the anxiety we feel in times of transition and trouble. And that's precisely where faith comes in. God's Word says we are to walk by faith, not sight (see 2 Cor. 5:7).

If fear is rooted in what we don't know, faith is rooted in *who* we know. Faith flows from a relationship with our loving God. Fear says, "I don't know what comes next." Faith says, "I'm connected to the One who does know and I trust Him completely."

Picture a small child alone in a large park. The child may feel "lost" even though Dad is just a few yards away watching the child closely. The child may feel alone and uncertain about what to do and where to go. The child may feel fear about how to get out of the park and back home to safety.

All of that fear and those feelings of being lost and alone change when Dad shows up and takes the child's hand. The child no longer needs to know all the details about which paths to take to get out of the park and back home. The child is holding the hand of the one who knows, and that is sufficient.

I frequently say, "The amazing thing about faith is that it functions most effectively in creative tension." Why? Because that's when we turn to God and reach out to take His hand.

The amazing thing about faith is that it functions most effectively in creative tension.

When everything is going well, we tend to do things on our own and we usually fail to seek His advice. Then, when a trial, trouble, or time of transition is upon us, we too often continue to struggle with the difficulty we are facing—on our own strength. We flail about emotionally, trying to get rid of as much tension as we can. Most people perceive tension or pressure as a bad thing, equating it with a sore neck, furrowed brow, or nagging headache. That isn't tension! Those are merely physical symptoms. Real tension can't be resolved with a muscle relaxant, a massage, or a long whirlpool bath.

True tension is the feeling we have when we know that a situation or circumstance in which we find ourselves is not "right." Perhaps the situation doesn't fit our concept of goodness, truth, beauty, or love. Perhaps the circumstance doesn't fit what we believe to be our rightful position in life, or what we believe about

God. Tension is the uncomfortable zone between what is and what we intuitively know might be or should be.

In truth, tension is a required part of the creative process in each of our lives. It is because of tension that we seek a better way, a better life, a better method. It is because we feel the tension of "not liking" what is around us that we seek to create something we do like. It is because of tension that we choose to walk out of our dark, dingy life and pursue a brighter future.

To say, "I want a full life but I don't ever want to experience tension" is like sitting in front of a fireplace and saying, "I want continual warmth in my life but no fire."

Tension drives us to creativity. It motivates us to action. It also drives us to faith.

At some point in our active pursuit of a creative new way to live, we all come up against the brick wall of realizing we can't do this solely on our own strength and power.

Oh, we try!

Do we ever try!

Many people spend most of their lives trying in their own intelligence, physical stamina, and cunning schemes to create the life they want out of the shards of the life they currently have. In the end, they find themselves exhausted, frustrated, and with no less tension.

Faith is reaching out for God's hand in the time of tension. It is saying, "I can't, God, but I believe You can. Let me link up with You and get into the flow of Your plan and purposes. I believe that You can help me live fully, freely, and fearlessly in the destiny You have planned for me. Help me to trust You every step and every day as You lead me into the fullness of who You created me to be."

Don't pray for tension to go away.

Instead, pray for God to *show you the way* to His purposes. When you are in the flow of what He has created you to be and do, you will experience the right amount of tension that empowers and enables you to succeed at the tasks He has put in your path.

Choose to look on the bright side of tension or pressure—especially as you are trusting God to move you forward and upward toward His highest purposes for your life, including fearlessness. See the proper amount of tension with new eyes:

- *Tension motivates us emotionally.* It causes us to move, to act, to decide, to choose, to get off dead center mentally or emotionally. It causes us to move toward what we perceive will be greater safety, justice, or pleasure.

- *Tension focuses our attention.* It causes us to target a specific problem and come up with specific solutions. It causes us to maintain concentration, and turn away from those things that would distract us or tempt us in negative ways.

- *Tension stimulates us.* A certain amount of tension gets us going and keeps us moving physically. The tension we experience when we are hungry or thirsty, for example, stimulates us to seek nourishment for our bodies.

Choose to look on the bright side of tension or pressure.

We benefit most when we allow tension to ignite our faith. When we feel tension, we are wise to say, "God, help me move, act, decide, and choose those things that are beneficial to my living out Your design for my life. God, help me stay focused on doing what is right—keep me from being distracted by anything that might harm, diminish, or hinder me, or keep me from the success You desire for me. Help me to say no to all temptations that will waste my time or resources or energy. God, give me the energy and strength I need to do what You have given me to do as quickly and as well as possible!"

TWO WAYS YOUR FAITH GUIDES YOU IN TIMES OF TRIAL

There are two important ways in which we need to use our faith to bend our fear as we walk through a time of trial.

1. A Precision in Timing and Methods

We must trust God not only to show us *what* to do but to show us clearly *when and how*. God alone knows the timing and methods for you to be positioned or to be launched into the fullness of your purpose. This sense of timing is related to but not limited to *kairos* time, which we discussed previously. This sense of timing is daily—it is a matter of knowing when to speak and when to be silent, when to act and when to refrain from acting, when to reach out and when to pull back. There is a rhythm to life.

Every actor or actress knows the importance of "hitting the mark" with a precision of timing. If an actor arrives on stage prematurely, he throws off all of the other actors and negatively impacts the storytelling. If an actor fails to hit his mark—standing and moving precisely where he was directed to stand or move—he will throw off the overall choreography and staging.

The same is true for our lives. Timing is critical. It is vital that you come to the place where you are willing to trust God explicitly for precisely when, how, and in what ways you should speak up or take action.

It is vital that you come to the place where you are willing to trust God.

I have watched many people who knew they had a call of God on their lives—a call intended for their success and fulfillment as they met a particular need or addressed a specific challenge—who failed because they acted prematurely.

Some have lost their finances.

Some have lost their families.

Some have nearly lost their minds.

Nearly all have lost a significant percentage of their enthusiasm about their own goals and purpose in life.

I have encountered literally thousands of women in recent years who are looking for a spouse. This is a natural desire and dream to pursue. We are created to desire a husband (see Genesis 3). The Bible tells us that a good spouse is valuable; and as we are well aware, things that are valuable are rare, and things that are rare are always hard to find. It takes time to find a truly good, suitable mate. Never assume that just because a person came riding into your life on what looks like a white horse, the person is the right one for you. First of all, the horse may not be their horse! And second, the person may not at all be interested in getting off that horse and settling down in your barn for a lifelong stay.

Ask God to reveal to you His timing and His methods. Obey Him. Remember the patterns of God are permanent. In Genesis, God reveals His patterns and order. He starts with position, then purpose, then person, then partner. We often try to get a "partner" before position and purpose. It's out of divine order.

2. Handling the Taunts and Threats of Bystanders

Faith also guides us through times of trial by giving us confidence to ignore the taunts and threats of bystanders.

We all know the children's rhyme: "Sticks and stones might break my bones, but words will never hurt me." It isn't true. Words *do* hurt us. The only way to walk with your head held high in times of taunts and threats from other people is to know you are holding tightly to the hand of the Almighty One who has promised to bring you to your intended purpose with full accomplishment.

Do not be naïve. As you walk your path toward success, you are going to encounter those who seek to pull you off. Sometimes they will simply taunt you, trying to divert your attention with inconsequential provocations, teasing, or mocking. I recommend that you ignore taunts and keep walking.

At other times, bystanders who see you walking toward success may threaten you. Threats are significantly different from taunts. Threats are an intention to inflict evil or cause damage. They are a "menace." They produce fear in us.

What is the power in a threat? Why do threats have more power than taunts? Because a threat always has an element or degree of truth in it. There's just enough truth in a threat to capture our attention. The element of truth is what we see from the outside — it is like a wrapper around a hard-core lie. The lie that is at the heart of any threat is a lie about our value, worthiness, or love-ability.

If you are feeling threatened today by someone, you need to decide: "I will not live in fear because of his threats. He may as well stop threatening me because his threats are going to fall on deaf ears from this day on." You may have to literally say that, or it may be an internal declaration that establishes healthy boundaries.

If there is a thought habit that amounts to an ongoing threat, you need to face that threat and determine what is the worst that can happen. And then, begin to see all of the various options and outcomes that might be possible in the wake of the worst possible answer. At all times, envision God lifting you up and carrying you through that worst-case scenario. By doing these things, you are eliminating fear from ruling and reigning in your life.

FAITH AND TRUST LEAD TO RENEWAL OVER TIME

Walking boldly and confidently by faith—fully exercising and using our spiritual minds—happens over time. It is a process.

The more we use our faith, the stronger it grows.

The more we use our faith, the stronger it grows.

The more we trust in God, the deeper our relationship with Him grows.

The more we apply God's Word to specific situations in our lives, believing fully that God's Word will work to bring about positive change, the more we will see changes that truly are beneficial and filled with blessing.

It is over time that our thinking becomes renewed, our attitudes are transformed, our beliefs are firmly grounded in truth, and our desires come into complete alignment and agreement with God's desires for us.

We cannot renew ourselves. We must set out to know God's Word and learn the character of God. We must believe God is for us, loving us and guiding us toward His good purposes. We must apply what we know to do, especially in matters of timing and methodology, and in the face of taunts and threats. It is as we do these things that the renewal process occurs within us as a normal, natural spiritual by-product. We become fearless. We move on, and we move up.

MOVING ON

Is there a specific fear or situation in your life
you need to confront with your faith?

MOVING UP

What is your understanding of the way God desires for
you to move through a time of trial or transition toward
His higher purposes for you?

9

Back to Your Future

Lili was not unlike many first-semester college seniors. She was facing graduation in a few months. She grimaced to herself that, unfortunately, she had not found her "man" yet, so she likely would be graduating to the job market, rather than to a wedding ceremony. She had enjoyed her studies in college, and would be graduating with a degree in business. She had no clue, however, what it was that she wanted to do with a business degree. The options seemed unlimited and she was nearly paralyzed in the face of them.

Start her own business?

Work for a mom-and-pop small business?

Seek employment in a major corporation?

And for any of the above, in which city and for which enterprise?

Lili went to the career planning and placement office at her university and left even more confused. She told a friend, "About the only thing I discovered is that I'm a morning person, not a night person, and I like to work with people only about half of the time—the rest of the time I like to work on my own. One of the tests said that I was good at working with my hands, and the other test said I was a good conceptual thinker! What am I supposed to conclude from that?"

Almost as a last resort, Lili went to see a former Sunday school teacher, a woman she knew had been successful in business but also was wise when it came to spiritual matters. This woman asked her, "What does your spirit tell you?"

Lili was puzzled. "I'm not sure I know what you mean."

Her teacher said, "Does your spirit tell you that you will succeed or fail?"

"Succeed, I suppose," Lili said.

"Of course!" her teacher replied. "You trust God and you know that He has success in your future, not failure. From the time I knew you as a seventh grader, you have had ambition and motivation. You set goals and expected to reach them.

"What else does your spirit say?" her teacher asked. When Lili didn't respond immediately, her teacher suggested, "I remember that you loved to do creative things as a young woman — you were always the one eager to help with party plans, including designing decorations and planning out the food and activities."

"Oh, I loved that!" Lili said, with great enthusiasm and energy. "We had some great parties in our Sunday school class back then!"

"Maybe that's what your spirit has known all along you should do — be an events planner."

That's exactly what came to pass. Lili moved to a large city to work for a firm that specialized in event planning for charitable organizations. In the next five years, she helped various organizations host events for up to three thousand people, raising tens of millions of dollars to help people in need.

She told her Sunday school teacher after the first five years of her job, "I was made for this. I couldn't be happier or feel more fulfilled."

What is your spirit telling you? In this time of moving on and moving up, you need to tap into this vital inner resource.

YOUR SPIRIT KNOWS EVEN IF YOUR MIND DOESN'T

Your spirit knows more than your mind, because your spirit is eternal. Your mind was created by God for you to make wise decisions regarding your relationship with Him, to solve practical earthly problems, and to make sound choices regarding the use of your time, material possessions, and physical energy. Your spirit was placed within you from eternity past to connect you all the way through your earthly life to your eternal future. Your spirit understands and is connected to eternal truth and eternal purpose. Therefore, your spirit carries knowledge of many things that your conscious mind cannot explain. In other words, you can know something apart from reason, or apart from having an ability to express what you know in words.

*Your spirit knows more than your mind,
because your spirit is eternal.*

The God of eternity has placed eternity in every person's heart. We are all saddened at the death of a loved one. Why? Because we want life to continue—we believe it should. However, real life is not this "blip on the radar screen" of the time we spend here on earth. Your birth certificate is simply when you clocked in to your purpose. According to Hebrews 9:27, there is a time for your purpose to be complete. "Just as man is destined to die once...." King James says "appointed." The word means to be reserved, laid up, made, and set. There is a time that has already been set for your assignment on earth to be complete. Of all God's creatures, we human beings are the ones who have a concept of eternal life.

I believe we carry a memory of the future in our spirits that our minds often struggle to comprehend. This makes sense only if we have an understanding that God is eternal. He alone sees the beginning from the ending of all things. As created beings made in the spiritual likeness of God, we also have a seed of eternity deep within us. We can remember the past, we can understand the present, and we have dreams and visions and prophetic insights into the future.

As "modern" men and women who are highly reliant upon technology and science, we rarely tap into the deep memories that were familiar to our ancestors and to more primitive people groups around the world today. These memories are passed down to us in subtle ways, including genetic ways, so that we respond to life *now* in a way that was considered important for preservation in the past and is also considered valuable for implementation of the future. We have a portion of God's heart and memory, which gives us a knowledge that transcends time and space.

God also gives us His Spirit, and the Spirit most definitely knows the visions God had, has, and will have for our lives. It is God who set us into the context of time, circumstances, and environment. But it is also God who created in us an unalterable purpose and a set of traits and abilities with which to fulfill that purpose. The Spirit knows God's vision for our lives and it is the Spirit who reveals God's vision to us.

THE BIG PLAN

In an earlier chapter I referred to the words of the Lord that the prophet Jeremiah voiced: "I know the thoughts that I think toward you, saith the LORD, thoughts of peace, and not of evil, to give you an expected end" (Jer. 29:11). This phrase in Jeremiah, "an expected end," might also be translated "hope in your latter end."

We are to anticipate our future with hope! In Jeremiah 30, God very clearly told His people what their end would include:

- Total defeat of their adversaries (v. 17)
- A lasting home (v. 18)
- Every reason for thanksgiving and merriment—joy to the fullest (v. 19)
- Many heirs (v. 19)
- A recognized identity and power on the earth (v. 19)
- Children who serve God (v. 20)
- Leaders who have a heart for God and also a heart for the people (v. 21)
- An unending relationship with God (v. 22)

Who doesn't long for these things in his or her life? This is the big-picture expected end God desires for us that we must come to desire for ourselves.

In previous days when we took photographs using film, we had to wait to see what we had intended to capture photographically. Sometimes film remained in the camera for days, weeks, even months until the entire roll of film had been shot. Was the image embedded on the film that entire time? Of course. Was the image capable of being seen by the naked eye? Not at all. In fact, if the film was stripped from the camera and exposed to viewing in the light, the image could be destroyed. It was only in a darkroom and after submission to very carefully balanced chemicals that the image was revealed on the film, and then, after more chemicals and processing, that the image on the film could be transferred to special photographic paper for accurate viewing.

In many ways, this is an excellent metaphor for God's purpose and vision planted on our hearts. God sees our fullness. He imprints His plan upon us. And it is as we submit ourselves to God's Word that

God's plan and purpose become revealed to us. As we begin to live out God's plan, we see and understand it with greater and greater clarity. We come to know ourselves even as God knows us. We become capable of identifying more fully who we are, why we are on this earth, and what it is that God still has ahead for us to be and do.

God sees our fullness. He imprints His plan upon us.

THE INDIVIDUAL PLAN

It is in the context of this Big Plan that God embeds His personal plan for us. It is important to recognize that nothing about His personal plan for us will negate or override the Big Plan. If you find yourself desiring a goal that is not in line with the big-picture goals God sets for all of His people, reevaluate your desire.

I remember as a high school girl going with my friends to San Francisco. They were into the club scene and liked to party and stay out all night. I preferred to look at the row houses with their beautiful bay windows. I said to my friends, "Someday I'm going to own homes like this."

They stared at me blankly. "Why?" one of them asked. I think they thought perhaps I wanted to be a Realtor.

"I'm going to have orphanages around the world," I said. "They'll function like homes in row houses—they'll have an administrative center but be a series of separate family-style units in connected living spaces."

I wasn't even a Christian at the time, but God's purpose was already embedded deep within me. At a very deep intuitive level I knew one of the things I would do with my life.

Think back to what you may have said as a child about what

you were going to do or be. I have never met a child who says, "I'm going to grow up and be mediocre," or, "I'm going to grow up and be a drug addict." I've never met a girl who said, "I'm going to be abused and then become a prostitute," or a boy who said, "I'm going to fail at every job I attempt to do."

Most young children I know—including those with whom I have worked in inner-city projects and poor rural areas across America—want to grow up to be moms and dads, live in their own homes, have friends, do work that they find enjoyable and satisfying, and have a pet cat, dog, horse. For the most part, those children who grow up in church expect to raise their children in church someday. Young children have no doubt that they can sing, dance, paint, or draw; learn; help out in meaningful and even important ways; and have ideas worth talking about. Young children know there are some things they are better at doing than other things, and that they can't or won't win every competition they enter. They enjoy competing nonetheless, and they also enjoy making friends and doing things in a cooperative way.

It is only later in life that children seem to be influenced by adults to believe that they are not creative, cannot achieve, and will never attain their dreams. By the time many people reach adulthood, they seem to have lost sight of their innate God-given talents, their personality-based abilities, and their spiritual gifts. What a sad loss! Like a forensic examiner, go back over your childhood and discover who and what you authentically desired.

Go back over your childhood and discover who and what you authentically desired.

Think back to what it is that you enjoyed doing as a child. What did you want to be? How did you want to live? What really brought tears of joy to your eyes as a teenager? What made you angry, with a sense that justice needed to be achieved on behalf of someone who was hurting or in need? What did you most look forward to doing?

When people in their thirties and forties tell me that they still don't know what they want to do with their lives, I often ask them, "What did you enjoy playing at being when you were seven or eight years old?" The games we enjoyed most as children, the areas of learning that most captivated our imagination and interest, and the activities that we were "good at" or "best at" are very often predictors of our God-given talents. It is the use of those talents in ways that benefit others that results in our greatest sense of purpose. A dear friend of mine knew from the time she was three years old and asked for a doctor's kit that she would be a physician. She is an amazing African American who faced many obstacles but refused to settle for anything less than her destiny and childhood dream.

I don't know your purpose, but I believe with all my heart that, deep inside, you know the purpose for which God created you. You may not have thought about your purpose. You may not yet have discerned it in your spirit and brought it to your conscious mind. But you have a purpose and you can discern it. It lies deep at your core. It is the fullness of your authentic self. And when you live it out, there is such satisfaction to life.

ABILITIES AND OPPORTUNITIES

God has gifted you with abilities. Some of us have one main ability, some a few abilities, some have many. We need to know our abilities. God has given them to us so we might develop them and use them.

Some of your abilities fall into the category of natural talents—perhaps a musical ability, an ability to work with your hands, or an above-average intellectual ability.

Some of your abilities are personality related—you may have a quick wit, an ability to make friends easily, an innate ability to nurture children.

And some of your abilities are spiritual. You may have an ability to discern right from wrong, to "read" people, or to gain insights into the Word of God. There are many other abilities you may never have considered, explored, or developed.

In addition to natural, personality-related, and spiritual abilities, God has given each of us opportunities. They come to us or fly past us daily. Situations. Encounters. Conversations. Appointments. Call them by whatever name you choose, God places you in circumstances and environments that have within them a potential to further or hinder your purpose in life.

Yes, God has placed within your spirit an intuitive, deep, spiritual understanding of your purpose in life. God put that in your spirit from the moment of your creation—it is as much a part of you as your physical DNA.

God has placed within your spirit an intuitive, deep,
spiritual understanding of your purpose in life.

THE ONGOING PROCESS OF DISCOVERY

This is a choice that will help you move up: work toward discovering your purpose as revealed in your spirit. I believe strongly that God will reveal His ultimate purpose to any person who seeks. God does not desire that we stumble through life but that we succeed at our "intended end" purposes. The details of that purpose, however, are an ongoing matter of discovery and applying our faith. Discovering the details of God's plan is an integral part of God's processing us.

From my late teens and early twenties, I knew—through a very real vision and confirming words from the Lord—that I had and continue to have a purpose to "speak to nations" and impact them spiritually, economically, and socially. I have had a clear awareness of that purpose for over twenty years. I have an abiding confidence that this is still my God-given purpose. But I also have an awareness that this is all I know about my purpose.

I don't know how all the facets of my purpose will unfold.

I don't know what timetable or which methods God may use next.

I don't know who God may bring into my life, what He might lead me to say to that person, or what the outcome might be. The destiny is clear, but the details continue to come forth.

At the time God first gave me that word about my purpose, I had no idea that I would work among the poorest people in the inner-city projects and neighborhoods of some of our largest cities, speak to the rulers of foreign nations, or mingle with some of the most influential and financially successful people in our nation. That's all been a matter of applying my faith to specific choices and decisions, and of discovering the details of God's plan.

The discovery process, for many of us, is discovering our authentic selves—the "real us" that has been there all the time. It is discovering our unique talents and abilities, tapping into our deepest desires, and beginning to dream again our greatest dreams. If you do not know the value of your authentic voice—who you really are and what you are to do with your life—I encourage you to read my book *You're All That!*

The faith process involves allowing God to trim away from our current life anything that is not authentic or not a part of our eternal purpose. Again, we experience creative tension as part of this process.

Most of us are living between nowhere and somewhere. "Nowhere" is everything that is not a part of God's plan for us personally. "Somewhere" is everything that is part of God's plan. We must allow God to lead us from our nowhere—which may include memories, habits, emotional patterns, and associations—to our somewhere, which has already been established in eternity. We must allow Him to cut away anything that does not conform to His highest and best for us.

Ask God to take you back to your future so you might have a clearer understanding of why you are going through your present struggle, pain, trouble, or transition. There's a purpose, there's a plan, and there's a good and expected goal!

MOVING ON

What is it that you wish you knew about yourself?

MOVING UP

What do you perceive in your spirit that God created
you to be and do?

10

Cut to the Designer's Pattern

Everybody at the retirement center and community admired Mildred's energy and focus. She got up every morning and went to work—right there at the retirement center—knocking on the doors of her neighbors to see what they needed. And then, she set herself to help in whatever ways she could. She had learned a phrase from her grandson that she used at least a dozen times a day: "You have to be intentional." Mildred didn't want anything in her life, or the lives of those around her, to fall through the cracks. She certainly didn't want to end her days in a "slump," as she called it—without purpose, without accomplishment, or without good friendships. She wanted an intentional life.

"Need anything?" she'd ask a neighbor. They knew her well enough to know that she wasn't just making small talk. Their needs filled her day with variety. On one day alone she reported that she had helped transplant three houseplants that had outgrown their pots, gone to the pharmacy to pick up two prescriptions for a neighbor too ill to go, called an agency to arrange for housekeeping services for a neighbor's dear friend who still lived in a house and could not fully care for it, helped balance a checkbook, and hemmed a skirt for a neighbor whose eyesight kept her from doing fine stitching.

A person once asked Mildred, "Don't you feel 'used' by some of your neighbors?"

"No," she replied bluntly. "If I know they can do what they are asking, I tell them that I'll go along for company while they run that errand or do that chore. Or I laugh and tell them that I'll expect to see that job finished when I call on them the next day." But then, after a moment of thought, she added, "So, what's wrong with being used? We're all supposed to be useful for something, aren't we?"

Indeed, we are!

GOD'S PROCESSING PREPARES US FOR OUR FULFILLMENT

Not only did God create us, but He continues to make and conform us to the pattern of our original creation. The truth is, many of us have messed up God's original design and we have gone off course from the intended purpose for our lives. We have chosen to do things our way, or we have blindly followed the suggestions of the media and others around us, and in so doing, we have tacked things on to our lives that detract from the core purpose of our creation. We have acquired bad habits, unhealthy associations, life patterns in our thoughts, emotions, and beliefs that are totally out of line with what God desires for us. We must allow God to strip away those things and redirect us toward the precise goal and destiny God established for us.

Not only did God create us, but He continues to make and conform us to the pattern of our original creation.

Not long ago God led me to study a particular passage of His Word. It dealt with the concept that we are being fashioned as arrows to be shot forth into the world from God's bow. God is the craftsman and the marksman. We are the workmanship of His hands.

An arrow does not choose its target. An arrow does not decide its direction or time of use. It is the marksman who crafts his arrows, determines their use, and shoots them with accuracy to hit a designated target for a specific purpose.

So it is with your life.

GOD IS THE CRAFTSMAN

God made you who you are. God built into you tremendous potential at your birth, according to a plan He had already developed for your life. He has created every waking moment of your life up to this moment. He has allowed certain people and experiences and circumstances to come into your life. He has allowed both tragedies and successes to impact you. He did not create you and walk away from you—the exact opposite is true! He made you and continues to make you.

To get a deeper understanding of this, consider what was involved in the making of an arrow in Bible times.

Arrows Were Made from Acacia Wood

This was the hardest wood known in Bible times—it was also called "iron wood" because it was so strong and impenetrable. This is the wood that was used in the construction of the Ark of the Covenant, the most holy vessel in Jewish history and considered to be the "seat" of God's presence on the earth. Acacia wood had enduring power and it was used for noble purposes.

You have a strength in you that you may never have acknowledged or embraced. You have enduring power. You have the capacity for being used by God in a profound and noble way.

How do I know this is so?

Because in many cases, people should not survive the things they go through!

It doesn't take much for people to recall their drug-using days or the times they recklessly drove while drunk. It doesn't take much to recall the abuse that resulted in broken bones or the injuries received during a gang fight. Even those who have lived good lives can look back and admit, "I should never have survived that heart attack...that burst appendix...that roadside bomb...that terrible car crash...that time of nearly falling down a steep ravine...that accident with the four-wheeler...that tour of duty in the military...that broken and bleeding heart."

Sometimes what a person goes through is emotional more than physical. He or she may have survived a serious bout with depression, hospitalization for mental illness, a devastating personal tragedy, a financial downfall that seemed irreversible, or an unfair public exposé that greatly damaged the person's reputation.

If God hadn't built strength into you, you wouldn't be standing. You wouldn't even be interested in knowing how you can grow to the next level God has for you.

You have areas of strength in you that are worthy to be recognized and developed. God has built into you the capacity to endure. He has created you to fulfill a good and noble role.

The Wood Was Cut and Sanded

An arrow maker cuts away anything that will keep an arrow from flying in a straight path. God also does this in His fashioning of us.

Are you aware that with your talents and abilities you could have pursued any one of hundreds of careers? You could have developed skills that would have qualified you to do any number of jobs.

Are you aware that with your talents and abilities you could have pursued any one of hundreds of careers?

Although you may never have consciously asked God to guide your life, He has done so nonetheless in profound ways. All through the years, He has been cutting away those things that were not according to His design and plan.

When it comes to the development of our character, God is always in the sanding process of our lives. His desire is that we reflect His own nature. He moves against anything that is contrary to our being the best we can possibly be.

All of God's cutting and sanding is to bring you into perfect alignment with His invisible and purposeful pattern for your life.

The Arrow Shaft Was Soaked in Water and Pinned

Throughout the Bible, water is a symbol of purity and cleansing. Water was used to soak clean the wood used for the arrow. God calls us to lives that are pure and cleansed of sin. The very essence of sin is autonomy from God, a failure to be dependent on Him. Sin is an integral part of our human nature. Romans 3:23 says, "All have sinned and fall short of the glory of God" (NIV). When we yield to sinful behaviors, they often momentarily escape or relieve but never truly satisfy our integral desires and longings. He has given us commandments that act as boundaries or borders for our lives—not to keep us away from things that are fun, but to safeguard us from those things that can cause us harm.

When we engage in activity that violates the principles of God to escape pain, relieve hurt, meet desires, or create an illusion, satisfaction, fulfillment, and acceptance, we only worsen our condition. The feeling of power over the pain created by "sinful behavior" causes you to repeat whatever will create that feeling again. Desire leads to need. Desperation leads to actions that will meet the need and because you are only satisfied temporarily, the action gets repeated and becomes a habit, something done so regularly and routinely that it is done without thought. And here is where the trap or cycle begins. That is why the Word of God says sin leads to death. It is not enough to simply change the behavior, but we must develop and have a strong, intimate relationship with God.

God desires that once we are cleansed, we remain cleansed—He gives us opportunity for ongoing forgiveness and renewal, always calling us to obey His voice and avoid the pitfalls that result when we err or rebel against His principles. He calls us to depend and rely on Him.

The Arrow Shaft Was Soaked in Oil and Repinned

Although acacia wood is very dense, it does have pores. And when an arrow shaft is soaked in water, those pores are open. That's the reason for soaking the arrow shaft in oil. The oil penetrates and fills the pores of the wood.

Oil in the Bible is a symbol for the Holy Spirit. It is the Holy Spirit poured into our cleansed lives that gives us the ability to make real spiritual changes and to experience spiritual renewal. The Holy Spirit functions within the boundaries of God's commandments—the Holy Spirit never inspires a person to do something contrary to the Word of God.

The Arrow Shaft Was Subjected to Fire and More Sanding

The fire and re-sanding assure that any excess oil has been removed from the outer surface. God's Spirit is intended to reside within us and give us personal strength and power in order to do God's work—the outpouring of His Spirit isn't intended for show or to impress others.

The fire also hardens the oil-soaked wood. It does not destroy or burn up the arrow, but it does prepare the arrow for long-lasting, multiple uses. Fire both purges and purifies us so that we are "good for the long haul." None of us is called to a one-day ministry. We are called to live out long, effective lives of service.

God tests us—He gives us opportunities to display our obedience. This isn't because God doesn't know our hearts; it is so we will know our own commitment. God's tests of us are not so that He can learn something about us. The tests are so we can learn something about ourselves and the strengths and weaknesses of our own faith and character.

God tests us — He gives us opportunities to display our obedience.

One End of the Arrow Was Ground to a Sharp Point

Arrows in Bible times were not crafted with flint or stone tips. The wood itself was sharpened to a point.

An arrow is not truly an arrow until it has a sharp tip. Until that point the arrow shaft is just a long, straight, narrow piece of highly sanded wood. Once the tip is ground into sharpness, the marksman has an arrow. The grinding process in your life is transforming you for your intended purpose. It's preparing you. To prepare means to cut in advance for something that has not happened yet. Like a seamstress who makes cuts and maneuvers to cut in alignment with the pattern, God is cutting some people, habits, and things from you during the grinding process.

Arrows Were Crafted with a Target in Mind

Marksmen in Bible times used arrows of three lengths, depending on the distance the arrow would be expected to travel. Arrows were also crafted with very specific targets in mind.

God is fashioning you to be very effective against a very specific enemy.

Countless enemies are active in our world today—some of them are forces of evil that exist in the invisible spiritual realm; others are very real enemies that can be identified readily in our natural and material world. Consider this list of rather high-profile enemies, which is far from comprehensive:

- Ignorance
- Poverty
- Illiteracy
- Crime—related to property, related to personal injury
- Repression—of ability, because of race, because of sex, because of social status, because of religion
- Slavery
- Genocide
- Wanton environmental destruction
- Disease
- Abortion
- Injustice

- Prejudice—racial, religious, social
- Abuse—physical, sexual, verbal
- Child neglect and abandonment
- Drug trafficking
- Depression
- Despair
- Brainwashing
- Faithlessness

All of us would no doubt agree that, at the very least, these are things our world would be far better without, and we likely would also agree that these evils are rampant in our world.

At some point in your life, God will choose to use you to confront evil in a practical, personal, and very direct way. Your life will find purpose and fulfillment when God shoots you as an arrow from His quiver against an enemy He defines.

At some point in your life, God will choose to use you to confront evil in a practical, personal, and very direct way.

A marksman pulls back the string on the bow in preparation for shooting an arrow. God pulls us back—very often He leads us to a time of withdrawal and preparation. Sometimes that withdrawal period is for fasting and prayer. Sometimes it is for reflection so that we gain clarity or a better understanding of methods. God releases us toward His target when *He* says we are fully prepared and ready. He sends us soaring with a divine accuracy. You can count on that!

KEEP YOUR FOCUS ON GOD'S GOALS

Throughout God's cutting away the extraneous things of our lives, keep your focus on the truth that God has a goal in mind! It's keeping your eye on the goal that allows you to make sense of your trial and endure it. A friend who is into dirt-bike racing told me that a basic rule of the sport is this: "Whatever you look at is where you go." If you get your eyes off the path ahead, you wipe out. This friend took his eye off the course one time. He put his focus on a rock instead of the path ahead, and he awoke strapped to a gurney and with bark in his teeth.

God has a purpose for you. He wants you to be useful. And it's in becoming useful according to His design, which involves sanding, fire, shaping, and sharpening, that you truly find your fulfillment.

MOVING ON

What are you doing today that is truly part of your eternal purpose on this earth?

MOVING UP

In what ways does God seem to be "remaking" your life for greater purpose?

11

Refined to Reflect His Glory

Brenda and Glenda were not twins, but they were sisters born only eleven months apart and were raised almost as twins. Their mother had put them into foster care and eventually had allowed them to be adopted after giving birth to three additional children—all of whom were born out of wedlock. Brenda, Glenda, and their three siblings each had a different father. At the time the girls left their mother they were seven and six years old.

Brenda and Glenda had been taken in and adopted by a wealthy childless family in a nearby town and had been raised with tremendous educational and social advantages. Their emotional needs, however, had never been fully addressed. Their adoptive parents believed fully that "nurture" would totally overcome "nature" and that their love would be sufficient to wipe out any early-childhood trauma.

Brenda, an average student, believed her adoption to be a great blessing. She took full advantage of everything offered to her and although she was not interested in going to college, she did go to a vocational-technical school and enjoyed a thirty-year career as a physical-therapy assistant. She later opened her own business as a masseuse. She married, had children, and became active in a small evangelical church. Her life was marked by faith and optimism. She had an abiding gratitude for her adoptive parents, and a compassion that led her to pray for her birth mother and unknown father. Those who know and love Brenda will tell you that she is a woman who seeks to make the most of every opportunity and who is patient and kind to all with whom she works. She is a loyal friend and loving mother and wife.

Glenda, the younger of the two sisters, was a brilliant young woman with many talents and abilities. Unlike her sister, however, she resented being taken from her mother and developed a sullen personality. As soon as she turned eighteen, she sought out her birth mother and went to live with her. She subsequently lived the life her mother had lived—poor, with several children and no marriage, and angry at society. She died in ill health as the result of diabetes complications when she was only forty-two. Her children remember her as a frustrated and disappointed woman.

Brenda had made a choice to live a better life.

Glenda had chosen to live a bitter life.

Nearly every person I know comes to a crossroads at some point during her life in which she can make the choice: better or bitter. The spiritually minded person who functions in faith will make the choice for "better." The enemy will always lead the carnally minded person toward bitterness, and estrangement not only from God but from other people.

Nearly every person I know comes to a crossroads at some point during her life in which she can make the choice: better or bitter.

The Bible tells the story of two of King David's sons: Absalom and Amnon. Amnon raped his half sister, Tamar. Absalom immediately began to plot against his half brother Amnon. One day he executed his well-thought-out plan against Amnon. The seed of bitterness that took root in Absalom's heart was not only against

Amnon but against their father, David, who, from Absalom's perspective, had done nothing to avert Amnon's behavior nor punish it. Absalom plotted not only the death of Amnon but the overthrow of King David.

This story of an entire family being ripped apart is one of the saddest in the Bible. Tamar lived in shame and solitude for the rest of her life. Amnon died. Absalom rebelled. And King David experienced a coup d'état and had to run for his life from Jerusalem. He chose to leave the city rather than fight his son; and even when Absalom waged war, David was concerned for Absalom's welfare and sought to extend mercy to him. In the end, Absalom died a horrible death—hanging from a tree by his hair and stabbed repeatedly by the swords of David's men. David returned to his throne, but not without much personal heartache and pain.

Each of the people in this sad tale faced the better-or-bitter choice. Only David made an ultimate choice for better.

The truth is this:

- As I've said, *what* you go through in life is not nearly as important as *how* you go through life.
- What you *accomplish* in your life is not nearly as important as the *character* you allow God to accomplish in you.

The things of great value in the sight of God are spiritual qualities of maturity, not outward material signs of acquisition. You may move on without spiritual maturity, but you will not move up.

THE TRAITS OF SPIRITUAL MATURITY

The most notable marks of spiritual maturity in God's Word are the following.

An Ability to Love

Love is giving—it flows from having received love and value from God. Mature people are givers. They seek to bring benefit to others, even more than they seek to benefit themselves. Selfish, hoarding, me-oriented people are immature when it comes to their capacity to love. True, mature love is selfless.

A Joyful Outlook on Life

An immature person seeks happiness. He continually says he wants to be happy and he looks endlessly for those things he hopes will make him happy. Happiness is situation-bound. It is related to circumstances and outer events, which are always in flux. The immature person needs more and more stimulation, and is in constant search of the next "new thing" that will create a feeling of being "high."

The spiritually mature person seeks joy, which is an inner quality. Joy is rooted in an awareness of the greatness of God and the many splendors of His creative work in a person's life. Joy flows from the inside out, apart from any external factor or situation. It is a mature person who knows that joy is not circumstantial. It is a mature person who can laugh at life's foibles, including his own idiosyncrasies and quirkiness.

A Peaceful Spirit

An immature person is restless, always looking for something to satiate the anxiety, fears, and restless yearnings of his heart. Genuine peace is a feeling of wholeness in a person's life that comes as a result of knowing that he is in right relationship with God and has an eternal destiny. Those who are spiritually mature have found genuine peace, even if the surrounding world appears to be falling apart. A mature person is able to ride out the storms of life and to maintain calm while others are in a panic. Such a person is steadfast and reliable. Such a person rarely feels the need to turn to outside substances to mellow out or relax.

Those who are spiritually mature have found genuine peace, even if the surrounding world appears to be falling apart.

Patience

Immature people want all of life in a gulp. They want the quick fix, a quick cure, quick meals, the quick and easy relationship, and quick success. They are impatient with others because at their core, they are impatient with themselves. They do not want to work or wait for what they want. Mature people have learned that long-lasting fixes and cures take time, slow-cooked meals are generally far better than fast food, relationships developed over time are more stable and more rewarding, and success is sweeter and more sustainable if it comes slowly.

An Attitude of Kindness

Immature people grasp. Mature people hold life a little more loosely—grateful for what they have, but refusing to cling to what is better given up or given away. Immature people are discourteous and arrogant. Mature people extend courtesy and allow for others to express their opinions and choices.

Good Character

An immature person may have the potential for good character and a modicum of good character, but a mature person is someone who has lived long enough to have reliably good character. Good character is marked by integrity, honesty, and consistency. It is impossible to evaluate the full depth of a person's character instantly or in one or two settings. Good character is revealed over time and in a variety of circumstances and situations.

Faith in God

The immature person trusts himself or relies on other people to be his benefactors. The mature person has learned that to trust oneself is folly and to trust others without question is naïve. The mature person puts his trust solely in God.

This is not to say that a person cannot believe for the best in another person. But an immature person sees only the best in people they like and rarely sees any potential for error, weakness, or fault. The mature person can believe for the best in another person, but at the same time, recognizes that all people make mistakes, have flaws, and manifest poor judgment.

A Humble Stance toward Others and God

Meekness is not weakness—it is controlled strength. Humility does not turn a person into a doormat for others. Humility says, "I am willing to be flexible enough to accommodate your good desires, and yet strong enough to express my own good desires." Before God, meekness is the attitude that expresses, "Not my will but Your will be done." The immature person is a me-me-me person. Immature people are proud, brash, and unyielding. A mature person is willing to compromise on matters of style and personal preference, and on all other things that are not eternal or vital to life.

Meekness is not weakness — it is controlled strength.

Self-Control

The immature person wants what he wants when and how he wants it. The mature person has developed willpower and restraint, and seeks what is best for all involved, in the ways and times that are most beneficial and appropriate.

Evaluate yourself according to these standards. Are you a spiritually mature person? Are you ready to respond to others in a mature way?

Evaluate a person you may be considering as a spouse or business partner. Is the person genuinely mature?

When in doubt, give yourself time to grow. Pursue character growth. If you have doubts about another person, give that person time to display his or her innermost qualities. Allow patience to grow in you as you wait for the timing of God.

A decision made in haste . . . just may produce wasted years and produce little return on the time and love invested.

STUFF YOU SHOULD LOSE AS YOU MOVE UP

There are things that will drag you down and keep you from flying toward your mark with accuracy and power. I cannot begin to fully describe for you all of the things that might fall into this category of things worthy to be shaken and eliminated, but here are some:

You May Need to Get Rid of Old Habits

Certain habits—from what you drink and eat, to substances you take into your body, to places you routinely hang out may be deeply engrained, but that doesn't mean they are either healthful or helpful to you as you face your future. Just because you've always done things a certain way, and you have come this far with that old habit, does not mean that this way of doing things is going to work best for you as you step into tomorrow.

You May Need to Shed Some Associations

Not every colleague, friend, associate, or acquaintance is someone who should be in your life. That person may have had a role in your past, and may be present today, but that doesn't mean the person is vital to your overall purpose in life. It doesn't matter that you may have grown up with them or once been best friends. If "Freaky Freddy" is now a drug dealer and Sally wants you as a friend only so she can use and abuse your time and compassion, then you need to say good-bye to them. Watch for the relationships that deplete you or take advantage of you.

You May Need to Shed Some Possessions

Not every investment you have made is one you should hang on to. Not every item you have purchased in the past is worthy of the time, energy, and expense of maintaining that item. Not every venture you have started is one you should continue. If anything detracts, distracts, or subtracts from your ability to move quickly, decisively, and boldly into your God-revealed future, you need to get rid of it. Donate it. Give it away. Pass it off to someone else who will benefit.

Your life is in a continual state of being restructured, remodeled, and—be encouraged in this—upgraded! Sometimes leaner is better. Less can be more elegant. Fewer can mean greater value.

Your life is in a continual state of being restructured, remodeled, and—be encouraged in this—upgraded!

A friend told me about helping an elderly person during a trip to Jerusalem. Their tour group was scheduled to walk on the ramparts of the wall that surrounds the Old City in Jerusalem. The steps up to the top of the wall are very steep. The older person looked at the steps and made two decisions.

First, she decided that she wanted to walk on the wall. She said, "I'm seventy-nine years old. I'm here. This is the only chance in my life I'm going to get to do this." Second, she decided that she couldn't get up those steps and carry all the things she had in her hands. She went back to the bus and left her purse, her bottle of water, her Bible, her notebook, her camera—everything but her passport, which she had in a plastic holder hanging around her neck. And then, she asked my friend, "Will you please push me from behind if I get stuck?" My friend laughed and agreed.

This woman—nearly eighty years old—took one step at a time, and she made it to the top. She continues to tell others to this day—more than a decade later—that the afternoon she walked on the walls of the Old City of Jerusalem was one of the greatest days of her life.

You face the same decisions this woman faced. Are you going to pursue what God has placed before you as the next step for your life? Are you willing to leave behind anything that might hold you back from taking that step?

You May Need to Shed Some Old Ways
of Thinking and Feeling

God will continue to come against any phobias you have—those fears have nothing to do with His design. He will continue to come against any prejudice you have against others because of their race, culture, age, or sex. He will continue to deal with you about your insecurities as well as any misperceptions or misconceptions you may have about Him!

In all of these areas, allow God to shake from your life those things that need to be left behind. Allow Him to burn off the dross that clouds your character. Allow Him to cut away any excess or any unnecessary aspects of your life that hold you back from becoming His perfect work. Don't be afraid to let go. God has a principle in His Word of "leaving and cleaving" (see Gen. 2:24). When He is calling you to leave something, it is because He has a greater thing for you to cleave to.

At the same time, allow Him to build into your life anything that is necessary for re-creating, reestablishing, and renewing you! Very often as God cuts things out of your life, He seeks to put into your life things that are good, pure, and wonderful—things that add new dimension and new quality to your life.

The end result of character "reshaping" is always a character that is better!

BETTER THAN EVER!

Some time ago, I was scheduled to speak at a very formal gathering of highly influential people. I had purchased a beautiful gown for the occasion. I had a strong sense that looking my best was a way of honoring the people to whom I would be speaking for the first time. Unfortunately, the gown needed some alterations and my schedule did not allow for me to go for a second fitting. The next time I put on the gown was minutes before arriving at the banquet hall. I was not at all comfortable with the alterations that had been made—the bodice was too low-cut. But what could I do?

I went to the ladies' room where I encountered a woman who was a stranger to me but who sensed my uneasiness. We began to talk and she let me know that she had designed clothes in the past and within a matter of a couple of minutes, we had removed one piece of fabric that seemed unnecessary and had positioned that fabric in a way that made the entire gown much more modest and appropriate—and more beautiful. The piece of fabric that had been "transplanted" was just enough to create an even more beautiful design.

Was the gown still a designer original? Twice so!

That's the way God works with us. He has a design for each of us. His design fits us perfectly. There is nothing out of place—nothing extraneous, nothing superfluous, and nothing missing. Sometimes we live in a way, however, that gets something out of place and our lives look inappropriate against the template of God's perfection. He sends us prophetic speakers and godly teachers to help us realign our thinking, feeling, and believing so that we are restored fully to God's original design. We are returned to our authentic selves!

The great news is that the more you allow God to refine you and design you, the better you are going to look—to yourself, and to the world. For a number of years now I have said to audiences, "I have looked into your future and you are looking a whole lot better in your future than you look right now." Audience members usually laugh at the way I say this, but they do not laugh at the truth of what I am saying.

The more you allow God to refine you and design you,
the better you are going to look — to yourself,
and to the world.

God's design for you is wonderful. It is original and glorious. And it *will* happen—faster or slower, sooner or later, to the degree that you are willing to allow it to happen. The future God has for you is beyond compare in its grandeur to your past or present. Indeed, you will be looking better in your future than you have ever looked before or look now!

MOVING ON

What character refinement does God seem to be
doing in your life right now?

MOVING UP

What kind of person do you want to be
remembered as being?

12

Practical Tactics in Times of Transition

Carla was nearly frantic. Her husband had told her the night before that he wanted her to go back to work after more than a decade of staying home to raise their children. "He's setting me up to divorce me," Carla confided to her friend Anna.

"What makes you think that?"

"Lots of things," Carla said. "He won't tell me where he's been when he comes home. I overheard him tell his friend Antoine, who is going through a divorce, that a man usually doesn't have to pay as much child support and alimony if the wife is working. He's been running up bills for personal things he wants—and I know he's setting himself up for taking bankruptcy after he divorces me."

"What are you going to do?" Anna asked.

That wasn't the question Carla wanted to hear. She wanted Carla to tell her how to keep her man, avoid going to work, and pray a miracle into her life. The truth was, both Carla and Anna had been praying for several years for Carla's marriage to improve. Carla and her husband had been to marriage counseling—but after only two sessions her husband had stormed out, saying that the counseling was nonsense and a waste of money. Carla was skilled and well educated, and her last child at home was a junior in high school. What more could be done that hadn't already been done or tried?

"I don't know," Carla finally replied. "I guess I'm going to go look for a job."

Carla's response to the impending trouble and change in her life was typical of that experienced by hundreds of thousands of women each year. Carla deeply held to her convictions about committed relationships, yet she faced the fact that others had a will free to make decisions that might violate that relationship. She knew that a time of transition was looming on her horizon, and everything within her resisted the idea.

I was caring for a sick child one day and the time came for the child to take a dose of medicine that had been prescribed for him. As I guided the teaspoon to his mouth, I said, "This is going to make you feel better. This is good for you!"

He grimaced as he took the medicine in his mouth and swallowed. "If it's so good for me, why does it have to taste so bad?"

I had to agree with him...the medicine tasted terrible.

We often feel that way, don't we? If transition and growth are good for us, why do we feel so bad?

The main reasons are deeply rooted in our human nature:

- As we've seen, we human beings are creatures of habit. We do not like change and we don't like the "unknown." All transition means leaving something we have known and reaching toward something we have never known and often can't see clearly. We resist change whenever and wherever possible.

Human beings are creatures of habit. We do not like change and we don't like the "unknown."

- When we human beings are faced with unknowns, we tend to fear the worst, not expect the best. Even though there's a

50 percent chance that things will get better instead of worse, we usually only anticipate what might go wrong, not what might go right.

- We human beings know that growth means leaving something behind. Change means a degree of loss. We don't like to lose. We count "losing" as painful.

All things considered, most of us do not want to grow. And if growth is required, we want it without loss or pain.

That simply isn't the way life works.

Rather than resist, God calls us to respond—and to respond with eagerness to His processing of us.

GOD CALLS EACH OF US TO A NEW WAY OF RESPONDING

The story of the children of Israel in God's Word gives us a tremendous example of each of these human qualities that are resistant to transition. For four hundred years, the Israelites knew a life of slavery and hardship. They knew what it meant to make bricks without straw, to endure plagues, and to be treated harshly and unjustly. Yet when the children of Israel found themselves miles away from Egypt, knowing they were heading toward a land flowing with milk and honey, they nevertheless began to whine, saying in effect, "We wish we were back in Egypt. We miss the foods we ate. We miss our homes. We're tired of manna, tents, and walking around in this sandy wilderness." They seemed to forget completely the pain of their previous years.

Millions of people around the world know the harshness of life—circumstances that are demeaning, conditions that are overly demanding, or situations that are devastating. They don't want to live in pain, but they don't know a way out. When a way out is revealed, they hardly know what to do. It is as if the door to the cage has been opened, but to step out of the cage is to enter an environment without boundaries, and with no clear understanding of the rules, expectations, or limits that might lie in the bigger world outside the cage. They feel tension as they transition.

They feel a sense of loss of the familiar, even if the familiar was bad. That is the reason so many people who are in abusive relationships return to their abusers. They don't want to hurt, but the sense of loss about what is familiar is more frightening to them than the severity of their past pain.

When a person moves from one city to the next, there is often a tremendous loss involved in the change of location—a loss of old familiar routes and habits, homes and neighborhoods, jobs and associates, and churches and places of recreation. Often there is a sense of loss related to friendships and family ties—the "loss" may be one of degree rather than the total loss of a friend or family member. The person who moves has less contact with old friends or family members, and in the early days of a move, very often has no contact with new friends or family members.

When a person divorces, there is transition and change, and very often, nearly overwhelming feelings of rejection, failure, and sorrow.

When a loved one dies, there is transition and change, and a tremendous loss accompanied by deep grief.

God calls us to come face-to-face with what it is that we truly are losing. That's the first step in identifying the purposes for our pain and for the transition in which we find ourselves.

IDENTIFY WHAT IS BEING LOST

When we find ourselves in times of transition, we need to do two things:

1. We Need to Turn to God and Ask Him to Help Us

We need to ask Him to heal our pain, give us insight into His work, and help us to transition with grace. Too often people blame God for their pain, rather than see Him as the source of healing for their pain. Don't reject God and run from Him. Turn to Him and ask Him to heal, restore, and comfort. He is the only one who can truly heal and restore you.

Too often people blame God for their pain, rather than see Him as the source of healing for their pain.

---

2. We Need to Identify What We Have Truly Lost

Over the years, I've counseled many women dealing with loss and pain. Sometimes the pain is so great it blinds us to what we've truly lost. We can't heal from what we can't identify. The following letter represents what I've heard from women who have discovered the power of a discerning perspective:

I spent about three months crying and moping around. I was hurting worse than I have ever hurt. I moved into a new apartment—which was all I could afford after taking a huge financial hit in the divorce—and I hated my new surroundings.

Then one day a friend showed up on my doorstep with a big bouquet of flowers. I began to cry and moan about all I had lost, and she was very blunt with me. She said, "Yes, I've been here the last ten years. I know some of what you have lost. Let's see—you have lost tirades of verbal abuse as your former husband told you all of your faults and blamed you for all of his failures. You have lost his angry outbursts that sometimes left you with a black eye or bruises. You have lost sleepless nights wondering if he would come home, and whether he would be drunk. You have lost hundreds of hours of worry about whether the telltale signs of lipstick on his collar and the smell of another woman's cologne on his jackets meant he was having an affair. You have lost even more hours of worry about whether he would be able to keep his current job, and whether he would overspend your family budget and leave you without enough money to pay the electric bill. In addition to all that, now that you live in an apartment, you have lost your sense of responsibility for keeping the lawn mowed and the pool cleaned—neither of which you enjoyed."

By the time she got that far, I was starting to smile. I got the point. After she left, I realized I had not fully discerned all of my losses! Some of those things I had lost I did *not* want to regain—ever. I had to figure out what was worthy of keeping and what needed to be lost for good.

After the children of Israel left Egypt, they moaned about no longer having fresh cucumbers and onions to eat. In looking back toward what they had left behind, they lost all sight of the fact that they had also left behind *slavery* and *bondage*! Their whining kept them from fully enjoying that their life of subservience to foreign people was now behind them. Ahead of them was a life of freedom and fulfillment and service only to a loving God!

Sometimes what is left behind may be good—there is nearly always *something* good about what is left behind. I certainly do not deny that. What I know, however, is that when God is in the time of transition and change, what lies ahead is always better than what was before. God's path for us is onward, forward, and upward. He doesn't take us from failure to failure. To the contrary! The Word of God tells us that He leads us from strength to strength, and from glory to glory. It is the pattern of God (Psalm 84:7).

When God is in the time of transition and change, what lies ahead is always better than what was before.

WITHDRAW, BUT ONLY IN ORDER TO ADVANCE

A number of years ago a person told me she was going on an "advance" over the coming weekend. I had never heard that term before. "An advance for what?" I asked. I thought she was going for a training session related to a new product prior to its public release. She said, "Well, you've heard of going on a retreat, haven't you?" I said, "Of course." Retreats are common in the church world—they are a needed and wonderful time to get new perspective on life and grow spiritually.

This woman went on to say, "Well, I'm not going to retreat from life. I'm going away this coming weekend to learn how to move forward in my life."

What a wonderful concept!

When we feel wounded or confused, or are in pain, our first response is to pull back. That is normal and acceptable. Even wounded animals often retreat into their caves or holes in order to heal after an injury. But rather than think of the time as a retreat or withdrawal, think of it as an advance.

The Bible has a number of examples of people who withdrew during a time of transition and pain. Moses spent forty years on the backside of a desert after he withdrew from Egypt and his life in Pharaoh's court. Paul withdrew for three years after his encounter with God on the road to Damascus. David withdrew for a number of years—some say as many as twenty years—after King Saul turned on him in a jealous rage. When Ruth found herself in Judea, she withdrew into a field to glean—a lowly position far from the normal social structure she had once known in Moab and away from the gathering of the women in her new hometown.

There's nothing wrong with withdrawing temporarily.

There's nothing wrong with retreating from trouble and pain for a season.

But don't retreat with an intent of making the retreat permanent.

Even in military campaigns when a contingent of soldiers is called to retreat, the withdrawal from the battlefield is rarely a white-flag full surrender. Rather, the time of withdrawal is for forces and equipment to be realigned and repositioned for a new attack. "Retreat" is tactical—it is skillfully planned for future accomplishment.

Don't waste your time of retreat. Use your time of withdrawal for healing and regaining even greater strength.

Each of the people mentioned above used their time of withdrawal as a time to heal and gain perspective, to regroup emotionally and spiritually, to redirect their focus, to renew their commitment to God, and to regain strength. Note those key words. They should be your focus when you are in transition and are feeling discomfort or pain.

Heal

Do what you know is good for you. Eat right, sleep sufficiently, exercise regularly. Stay in contact with close friends and get wise counsel. Stay involved in your church. Immerse yourself in the Word of God. Pray regularly and listen for God to speak in your spirit. Get outside of yourself and help others.

Regroup

Set some goals for yourself physically, spiritually, emotionally, and intellectually. These do not need to be earth-changing goals—set small goals that you can accomplish. For example, set a goal to take a ten-minute walk each morning, drink a protein smoothie every afternoon, read a few chapters of a book each day, or enroll in a class, Bible study, support group, or therapy group. Use your withdrawal time to draft a plan for the weeks and months ahead.

Redirect

Take charge of your thought life. Watch closely what you read, see on television (or as a movie or DVD), and attend. Keep your focus mentally on those things that are good, pure, wholesome, and beneficial. Engage in activities that require your total concentration in a positive way. Think of the things that bring you pleasure and peace.

Keep your focus mentally on those things that are good, pure, wholesome, and beneficial.

Renew

Spend time with God—long, soaking, uninterrupted, intimate time.

Regain

Establish new disciplines for your life that will put you on a path to greater strength. Very often in times of transition, there are good and sometimes necessary reasons to revamp your personal financial structure and to review all of your memberships and affiliations, perhaps needing to drop some and add others. Get good advice from a life coach or financial mentor who is grounded in the values you hold as your own. Put the same principle to practice in areas of your life that need restructuring.

If you will use your retreat time in these ways, you will find that you truly do advance.

Moses came out of the desert to lead the children of Israel out of Egypt.

Paul came out of his withdrawal period alive with the gospel message and prepared for his first missionary journey.

David came out of the caves of the Judean wilderness to become king.

Ruth came out of the field where she was gleaning to become the wife of the field owner, and the mother of a baby who would be the grandfather of King David.

Recognize that as you withdraw during a transition time, it is ultimately God who is "pulling you back" for His purposes to be accomplished. Those purposes involve what God will do *in* you, and eventually, what God desires to do *through* you. At times, His purposes are to keep you out of the way for those things He desires to do *around* you.

You may think that the wounding rejection, painful insults, or hateful actions of others are what have caused you to withdraw. David no doubt felt that way. He had done nothing intentionally or overtly to cause King Saul to throw a javelin at him or order his death.

You may recognize that your own improper behavior is what caused your withdrawal. Moses withdrew after murdering an Egyptian who had mistreated one of Moses' fellow Hebrews. God will still use it.

You may find yourself in a circumstance that led to your withdrawal, with very little conscious decision making on your part. Ruth perhaps felt this way. The death of her husband and her loyalty to her mother-in-law, Naomi, took her out of Moab and into a foreign land.

You may even find that you are caught up in a sequence of events that seemed to spiral out of your personal control. Paul was lowered down over a city wall in a basket so that he might escape a city that had become hostile to him after he turned from a zealous Christian-killer to a zealous Christ-confessor.

In the greater reality of God's plans and purposes, however, it is not the actions of others, circumstances, or some nebulous act of inevitable "fate" that causes you to withdraw during a time of transition and its related pain. It is God Himself calling you to a time apart with Him. His purposes for your withdrawal time are for your future good.

Withdrawal is not an act of cowardice. It is merely an acknowledgment of what is happening—change is occurring, transition is happening, process is proceeding.

Cowardice is staying in the cave long after healing has occurred and perspective has been gained.

Cowardice is staying in the cave long after healing has occurred and perspective has been gained.

God does not call you to remain withdrawn. He always calls you to withdrawal so He might prepare you for outreach and for moving into new territory. He is repairing, restoring, renewing, and reviving you for the grand future that lies ahead of you.

LOOK FOR THE BENEFITS YOU MAY NOT HAVE SEEN

A young person I know was recently offered a contract for a good job in an outstanding corporation. She pored over the contract in detail. I asked her what she was doing and she said, "It isn't just a matter of salary or the potential for advancement down the line. I'm looking for all the benefits I want."

We are wise to look for the benefits that can be ours. The hope of benefits can motivate us to submit to God's processing and to do our part in preparing for growth.

We should also recognize that there are desirable transition times, ones we can look to with great expectation. These are generally transition times with high potential for personal benefits and rewards, such as going away to college, changing jobs, moving to a new city, getting married, having a child, getting a new home, and so forth. Just because we want these transitions does not make them easier. It does mean, however, that our discomfort is offset from the start by a degree of joy and hope.

Certainly a person who goes away to college may have a degree of discomfort about leaving behind old friends and family members, but there's also the joy and hope of a new challenge, new friends, and a better life in the future.

A person who marries will have a degree of discomfort in adjusting to a new life of sharing and mutual commitment, but there's also the joy and hope of a loving relationship. A couple that has a child will have a degree of discomfort, not only in childbirth, but in the hours of child-raising—everything from two o'clock feedings to scraped knees to fights on the playground to episodes of rebellion. But there is also the joy and hope of a new life and an enlarged family circle of love.

The truly painful or distressing transitions are those instigated by others or that are the result of unforeseen circumstances. They hit us without our having an advance sense of joy and hope. The sudden loss of a job... the unexpected diagnosis of a life-threatening disease... the news of a terrible accident... the unanticipated demand for a divorce... the sudden death of a loved one... all of these and countless other circumstances can thrust a person headlong into an unwanted transition, out of which very little good appears possible.

In these times of transition, people often have a sense of being caught up in something that is beyond their control. Few things are more unsettling to most of us than being not in control. Being "not in control," however, is not the same as being "out of control." We do not need to let undesirable or unforeseen transition times throw us into a downward spiral or take away the hope and joy of life. Yes, the "landscape" of your life may change, and that change may be drastic, but you still have "life." Life is a gift given to each of us. Because something is not the same as it was before does not mean it is bad; it simply means it's taken on a new nature, form, or quality. It's up to you to discover the "beauty" of each season in your life.

It's up to you to discover the "beauty"
of each season in your life.

Not long ago I heard about a young woman who was participating in a normal, traditional, fun activity at a college. There was no sin, no rebellion, no reckless behavior, and no hazing involved. But there was a freak accident. The young woman suffered a severed spinal cord and became paraplegic. This young woman's life—and the lives of her entire family and large circle of friends—was thrust into a time of transition. There was much pain...and very little cause for hope or joy to offset it at the time, other than the fact that the injury was confined to her lower body. The good news was really less bad news—she wasn't going to be a quadriplegic and she wasn't going to die.

What should have been a normal start of a college career for this young woman—and a normal letting go of parents as a child entered a new joyous stage of maturity—suddenly became an unwanted and pain-filled transition time. Like this young woman, most of us will experience some unexpected life events during our journey.

What are the questions we are wise to ask in such a time of "undesired" transition? I believe the three most important questions to ask are these:

1. Is there opportunity for growth in this transition?
2. Is there an opportunity to display genuine faith in God?
3. Is there the potential for purpose in the new life ahead?

The answer to each of these questions is always a resounding *yes*!

We must never lose sight of the truth that God's nature is love. He always acts toward us with a motive of love. Therefore, we can know with certainty that God will never allow anything into our lives that is not ultimately for our eternal benefit. Again, I stress that God does not send all things but He uses all things.

Know refers to deep intimacy, an assurance, confidence, and understanding at the very core of a person's being. It is only when we truly know God and know that His purposes are for our good that we can trust God in all things.

Now, at times, we certainly would like for the outer circumstances of our lives to change dramatically. We cannot imagine that God has allowed such tragedy or trouble to strike our lives, nor can we imagine that His motive may be loving or His purposes may be for good. Everything within us cries, "No, not this!" I know. I've been there.

Even so, the truth—the sum of all our knowing that is accurate about the nature of God—is that God can and often does use very negative outward circumstances as part of His loving refinement of us for good.

As difficult as it is for us in our finite human minds to comprehend these truths, they remain true nonetheless:

- What we sometimes see as a burden, God sees as a benefit.
- What we tend to see as a weakness, God sees as an opportunity for His strength to be revealed.
- What we see as failure, God sees as fertile soil to plant seeds of success.

What we see as failure, God sees as fertile soil to plant seeds of success.

Remember God's individual purpose is to form you into the image of Christ, not to "fix" your external situations. "Real life" is from the inside to the outside, not vice versa.

YES, YOU CAN

Every time you hit a snag, a rough spot, or an unwanted "surprise," run toward God, not away from Him.

The Bible tells the story of a time when a great king and warrior from Assyria attacked Israel from the north. King Hezekiah heard about the victories of this man, Sennacherib, and he immediately tore his clothes and covered himself with sackcloth—a sign of great repentance. Then King Hezekiah went to the house of the Lord and called upon the scribes, the elders of the priests, and the prophet Isaiah. He said, "This day is a day of trouble, and of rebuke, and blasphemy; for the children are come to the birth, and there is not strength to bring forth" (2 Kings 19:3). King Hezekiah called upon those who served God in His temple to pray.

Hezekiah knew that his people were feeling weak in the knees at the very idea of Sennacherib's invasion from the north. The Assyrians were an especially cruel people, and their tactic was to wreak terrible pain and sorrow on their enemies, and then to take a significant portion of the conquered enemy—usually women and children—back to Assyria for assimilation. Those who refused to assimilate were tortured or killed. The Israelites in Judah were frightened and their fear weakened their resolve and eroded their faith.

Fear is the true enemy of faith. Doubt is not the opposite of faith, as many people believe. Doubt and belief are acts of the mind. Faith is rooted in the spirit—in the emotional core of a person and at the center of a person's values. Fear is what ravages our emotions and our values. Fear is what causes our faith to become paralyzed and ineffective. When you are struck with deep fear, recognize that you are facing a faith challenge. The time has come for you to rise up and declare, "I will trust God in this! I have an assured reliance on His character, ability, and strength."

Hezekiah stated very forthrightly that he and his people were facing a day of intense trouble...and blasphemy. He was not in the least bit of denial about the coming assault, nor was he in denial about his feelings and those of his people. Fear had a stranglehold on the land. Perhaps even more importantly, Hezekiah recognized that the attack was not only against the people of Judah—it was against the God whom the people worshiped in Judah. The Assyrians worshiped false gods and engaged in worship practices that were abhorrent to the Jews. That is what made their invasion an act of blasphemy.

We must never lose sight of the truth that when we who are believers in God are attacked by an enemy that does not believe in God, God is also being attacked. God does not abandon us when we are attacked. He stands with us. The attack is as much or more against the God we serve, and the good and right principles in our lives, as it is against us personally.

Hezekiah concluded that the time had come for his people to rise up and give birth to a tremendous "offensive" effort—to birth something new and powerful, but they were so weakened from the inside out that they did not have what it would take to confront Sennacherib's army. His statement was not a statement of remorse nearly as much as it was a statement of utter and total dependency upon God for strength and help.

It is one thing to say, "I can't" and to collapse in despair.

It is an entirely different thing to say, "I can't, but You can, God" and rise up in faith.

There is nothing in God's Word that ever calls upon a person to rise up and act on his or her own personal strength to defeat an enemy. In fact, the very opposite is true. God desires that we call upon Him in our time of trouble and that we rely upon Him for strength, wisdom, and supernatural intervention. God can and will carry you through any difficulties you face in life.

*God can and will carry you through any
difficulties you face in life.*

When young David rushed toward Goliath on the open battle-field between the armies of the Philistines and the armies of Israel, he ran with a shout:

> Thou comest to me with a sword, and with a spear, and with a shield: but I come to thee in the name of the LORD of hosts, the God of the armies of Israel, whom thou hast defied. This day will the LORD deliver thee into mine hand; and I will smite thee, and take thine head from thee; and I will give the carcasses of the host of the Philistines this day unto the fowls of the air, and to the wild beasts of the earth; that all the earth may know that there is a God in Israel. And all this assembly shall know that the LORD saveth not with sword and spear: for the battle is the LORD's, and he will give you into our hands. (1 Samuel 17:45–47)

David didn't rush toward Goliath in his own strength—he ran with God's strength. This is how we are to face every "enemy" encounter in our own life, with and by the strength of our almighty God. He was aware in every cell and fiber of his being that God was in him, with him, and all around him. I feel certain that nobody had ever spoken to Goliath in that way before. And in the end, David spoke a word of prophetic truth. Things came to pass exactly as David declared they would.

Perhaps this experience is what led David later to write so often and so eloquently in the Psalms about his utter dependence upon the delivering power of God. Here is just one of those psalms:

LORD, how they have increased who trouble me!
Many are they who rise up against me.
Many are they who say of me,
"There is no help for him in God."
But You, O LORD, are a shield for me,
My glory and the One who lifts up my head.
I cried to the LORD with my voice,
And He heard me from His holy hill.
I lay down and slept;
I awoke, for the LORD sustained me.
I will not be afraid of ten thousands of people
Who have set themselves against me all around.
Arise, O LORD;
Save me, O my God!
For You have struck all my enemies on the cheekbone;
You have broken the teeth of the ungodly.
Salvation belongs to the LORD.
Your blessing is upon Your people. (Psalm 3:1–8 NKJV)

What an example David and Hezekiah are for us when we are struck with trouble. It is in that very hour that we need to be at our strongest and most creative best...and yet it is in that very hour that we feel the weakest and most inept. It is in that very hour that we need to recognize that God is with us, that the attack against us is also an attack against Him, and that He is the source of our strength and our victory.

Read what the prophet Isaiah sent back as a word to Hezekiah: "Thus shall ye say to your master, Thus saith the LORD, Be not afraid of the words which thou hast heard, with which the servants of the king of Assyria have blasphemed me. Behold, I will send a blast [of hot wind] upon him, and he shall hear a rumour, and shall return to his own land; and I will cause him to fall by the sword in his own land" (2 Kings 19:6–7).

Here's How You Can

God has all the resources in hand to defeat those who come against you and seek to keep you from fulfilling your God-given purpose on this earth. He has all the resources necessary to deal with those who have hurt you or caused you to enter a time of intense trouble. To accomplish this, God can use and control *all natural resources, the information your enemy receives,* and *the outcome*:

All natural resources. The desert winds of the Middle East can be scorching—they completely debilitate a person's strength, even as they kick up enough dust to be blinding. A blast of hot wind became Sennacherib's immediate enemy.

The information your enemy receives. Sometimes God invades the thoughts and dreams of an enemy. Sometimes He causes a misperception or an inaccuracy to flourish in a way that creates confusion in an enemy's mind. The Bible says that the enemy of our souls, the devil, is the father of all lies, but we must never lose sight of the fact that God is God over the devil. The devil is subject to and limited by God. God can cause the lies of the enemy to become warped and boomerang back into the ears of an enemy. Whether God spoke directly to Sennacherib, or whether God used rumors from his close associates, the net effect was this: rumors coupled with a blast of wind from the desert, caused Sennacherib to turn around and head for home.

The outcome. God is ultimately in control of all things at all

God has all the resources in hand to defeat those who come against you and seek to keep you from fulfilling your God-given purpose on this earth.

times. Never lose sight of that truth. There is a God. God has a plan. That plan is always working and you are part of His plan.

You may think you are in control of all things at all times. In actuality, you control very little in your life. You do not control the most basic of your life's functions—you cannot make your heart beat another beat, nor can you make your lungs inflate for another breath. You cannot add a quarter of an inch to your height, nor turn back the hands of time to erase your past. You cannot predict with precision all the details of your future.

The government certainly isn't in control of all things. The devil isn't in control. "Fate" isn't in control—whatever your concept of fate may be. God is the Creator and He is also the Controller of your surrendered life. He is the One who authorizes good into your life. He is the One who controls the flow of difficulty in your life—so you can grow from it, become stronger as a result of it, and be changed by it in positive ways. Trouble is your servant by the hand of a sovereign God.

God not only sent strong words of encouragement to Hezekiah, He also let Hezekiah know exactly what He had planned for the wicked forces that were coming against God's people:

This is the word that the LORD hath spoken concerning him [Sennacherib]; . . .

Because thy rage against me and thy tumult is come up into mine ears, therefore I will put my hook in thy nose, and my bridle in thy lips, and I will turn thee back by the way by which thou camest. (2 Kings 19:21, 28)

God's word against the person or the forces that seek to devastate you and keep you from fulfilling His design for your life will always be a word of *destruction* to their plot against you.

God's word to you as His faithful follower will always be a word of *encouragement*.

God's word to you as His faithful follower will always be a word of encouragement.

There is nothing to be gained by denying yourself the strength of God's presence, wisdom, and encouraging love. Trust in and fully rely upon His power in you to overcome.

MOVING ON

What are the true losses you are facing? Name them all.

MOVING UP

What are the true benefits you may be gaining as you change and grow? Identify all you can see.

13

Validate Your Own Value

Mandy immediately went to her physical education teacher after she opened her report card for the semester. "I'd like to talk to you about my grade," she said confidently.

The teacher picked up her grade book and opened to the class in which Mandy had been enrolled for a volleyball class. "Yes?" she said.

"I think I deserve an A instead of a B," Mandy said.

"On what basis?" the teacher asked.

"I only missed class once, and that was administratively excused," she said matter-of-factly. "I was one of the best players in the class and was chosen to be a team captain. My team won the tournament at the end of the semester. And you personally asked me to be part of the school's official volleyball team because you thought I was a good player and a good leader. I believe that qualifies me for an A," she said with confidence, but without any tone of pride or confrontation.

The teacher looked at Mandy with a smile and then consulted her book. She placed a ruler on the line on which she found Mandy's name, and said slowly, "I believe you are right, Mandy. I was looking at the wrong line when I submitted your grade. Oh my, there's no telling who else I gave an incorrect grade. Thank you for bringing this to my attention."

Mandy knew her performance and her attitude had been right. She was happy the teacher agreed!

I once asked a young girl in the inner-city projects what she was good at doing. She said, "I'm good at reading and I'm good at playing jacks, but I'm best at jump roping."

Both this young girl and Mandy had healthy appreciation for their own abilities. They were able to self-validate their performance. What admirable traits to discern your value with confidence and not arrogance!

How good are you?

Go ahead, tell me!

Admit to me the areas where you shine. Describe for me the brilliance you display when you are truly in your groove and are working your stuff!

How good are you?
Go ahead, tell me!
Admit to me the areas where you shine.

Do you feel embarrassed or self-conscious distress to acknowledge your own greatness?

If so, you are like many people I meet. They don't want to talk about their strengths or their successes because they think it is wrong to "brag." They believe boasting is a sign of pride.

That all depends, of course, on whom you credit for your goodness and greatness. If you think that you have achieved anything solely by your own strength, intelligence, or cleverness, then you are bragging or "self-glorifying." If you believe you have accomplished all things because God both enabled you and empowered you to do so, then you are not bragging about yourself—you are bragging about God and His work in and through you. He is worthy of your praise. So go ahead and tell me, how good has God made you to be? Remember, He is the Creator and you are His creation.

VALIDATE YOUR VALUE ACCORDING TO GOD'S VALUATION

I have found in recent years that literally thousands of women—perhaps millions—do not value themselves correctly. This tendency is especially prevalent during seasons of intense pain. Most of those who err in their own value greatly underestimate their value. They often have bought into the "lies" and labels of life.

Our true value is not what *we* say about ourselves. Our value lies in what *God* says about us. God's Word gives a picture of an ideal woman who fulfills many roles: "Who can find a virtuous woman? For her price is far above rubies" (Prov. 31:10). In other words, a good woman is exceedingly valuable. God's Word also says on regarding a woman who becomes a wife, "Whoso findeth a wife findeth a good thing, and obtaineth favour of the LORD" (Prov. 18:22).

The truth here is that when God fashions a woman after His design and she lives out her authentic self, He makes her so valuable that nobody can "buy" her. If a man can buy you with fancy gifts or with fancy words, then perhaps you haven't allowed God to process you long enough. If another person can buy you with compliments or charm, you probably don't understand who made you. I encourage you to stay in His divine processor a while longer to see more fully how valuable you are. Therefore, you won't sell yourself short of your value. God's Word tells us that the only way a man can find and obtain a good wife is through "favor" from the Lord. It is God who allows a man to win the love, respect, and admiration of a good woman. Remember, the Bible declares, "What *God* has joined together..." (Mark 10:9 NIV, emphasis added).

So many women want to be wives so they can be "taken care of." They think very little about the care they will be required to give. It is only someone who has been through the processes of God who truly knows how to give and to care. The nature of love is giving and selfless.

What you catch is what you keep. Don't think you can "catch" a man and then change him. At the same time, don't think that if you catch a man, you will automatically become a good wife to him. Get yourself ready to be a "good thing"—totally and uniquely and authentically a good thing, regardless of any relationships you may or may not have. Then and only then can you truly be a "good thing" to the one God will join you to.

Some of the most valuable carpets on earth are those made in Turkey. The finest Turkish carpets have literally hundreds of knots per square inch. Most of these carpets are made by teenage girls, because only their fingers are nimble and strong enough to tie that many knots as finely as they need to be tied. It can take a young woman three to four years to complete one carpet, working long hours each day. The Turks have a saying that a man should not marry a woman until she has completed a carpet. What tremendous wisdom lies in that statement! A woman who has disciplined herself and has been steadfast in working at a fairly tedious task day after day and year after year, to complete something beautiful and lasting, is a woman who knows how to be patient and do the daily work of creating a long-standing relationship. The hours of knotting have produced something valuable in her character. Choose to prepare yourself with patience. Take the time to invest in yourself the things that will increase your "value." It is well worth the investment. We tend to take better care of things we perceive as valuable. We treat and care for them differently. Valuable things are not generally mishandled or discarded.

Take the time to invest in yourself the things that will increase your "value."

Are you aware that the most valuable things on this earth are things that are one of a kind? They are "originals"—never before created and impossible to copy exactly. They are rare. As I've said before, God has built into you a unique combination of amazing qualities that give you one-of-a-kind value.

Embrace and develop what God has designed into you. It sets you apart, establishes your value, and keeps you moving up.

RECAPTURE A VISION FOR YOUR FUTURE

Not only has God given you talents, abilities, and a personality that add up to your uniqueness, but He has placed within you and every other person a dream. A dream is a God-inspired hope and expectation made real to a person's imagination by the Spirit of God.

Take some time to revisit that dream. It lies at the core of your authentic self.

What is it that you used to dream of accomplishing, achieving, establishing, or doing? What is it that truly excites you and gives you an *I-can-hardly-wait-to-get-up-tomorrow-morning* feeling?

We sometimes dismiss imagination as involving only fantasy or whimsical daydreams. Some people even speak against imagination as being rooted in evil. That is far from the truth. That isn't the fullness of what God's Word teaches. God has given us the ability to imagine so we might be able to see in our minds and hearts a reality that doesn't yet exist; and therefore, we might begin to believe for, hope for, and work toward what God desires. God plants His dream in your heart by the Spirit of God, and He makes that dream blossom and come to life in your imagination. What you see is what you can be!

It is in your imagination that God allows you the opportunity to look beyond your present reality into the future He has already prepared for you.

It is what you can see that predicts who you will become.

Let me assure you of two key truths about your God-given dreams and your future:

1. Your Dreams Are Directly Related to Your Destiny

Your destiny is not framed by what other people do, say, or dream for you. Your destiny is defined and framed by what *you* do, say, and dream for your own life. Your destiny isn't limited or expanded by others. It is fashioned according to the truth of God's design for you and the way you put your goals and plans in alignment with His design. If you don't have a dream for your life, be assured of this: God has a dream for your life! Ask Him to reveal it to you.

2. Your Dreams Are Closely Linked to Your Desires

God promises to give us the desires of our hearts (see Ps. 37:4). But the amazing thing is that our deepest desire — the desire that is at the very core of our hearts and that will satisfy us to the greatest degree — is a desire that God has placed there. Our greatest desire is ultimately what our great God desires for us. The things that will be most fulfilling and meaningful to us are the things that God has built into us, brought to their fullest meaning.

Too often we think that some *thing* is what we desire. But things rust and break and wear out.

Too often we think that some *person* or a particular relationship is what we desire. But people disappoint us and all relationships end eventually—in death and a variety of other ways. There is great value in the right relationships but not complete fulfillment.

If you do not know your own deepest desires, ask God to reveal to you your own heart.

If you do not know your own deepest desires, ask God to reveal to you your own heart.

TAKE FULL ADVANTAGE OF ALL RESOURCES AVAILABLE

Once you have a clear dream for your life and you know the desires of your heart, begin to take full advantage of *all* the resources available for you to turn those dreams and desires into real goals, plans, and accomplishments.

Every person who seeks to grow and develop into the fullness of their God-created potential is a candidate for more information and increased skills. The resources are readily available, usually in a wide number of formats.

Go to a good bookstore that has both a large periodicals section and reference-book section. You likely will be amazed at the diversity of materials you discover. The topics cover serious subjects as well as hobbies. Today's reference books go far beyond encyclopedias or dictionaries—many are highly detailed and in-depth books that are written in easy-to-read language. You'll also find dozens of manuals and books that fall into the "For Dummies" or "Idiot's Guide" series—some of them address truly fascinating topics!

Read the headlines and first paragraphs of articles in a daily newspaper. You'll be amazed at the breadth of information you find there.

Check out the more serious channels on television. The science, biography, and history channels air dozens of interesting programs that are far more beneficial and just as entertaining as prime-time network programs (and generally without the sexual innuendos or images of violence and crime).

Don't just surf the Internet—take advantage of the information you can download or view on the Internet as a means of personal growth. What an amazing research tool this is for us today! Don't just use your computer to send mail or play games. Use it as an instructor.

Enroll in a short course at a community college, a local art gallery or museum, or perhaps your church or synagogue.

Seek out a Bible study or practical-church-living course that may be offered at your place of worship.

Ask an expert in a field of your interest to recommend a reading list to you, or to meet with you for an hour. Interview this expert about ways in which you might become more skilled or better educated in the field. Always value their time and confirm the access of relationship with gratitude they can feel.

Seek out a mentor or a life coach—someone who can pour into you periodically to guide your growth and development, perhaps in a particular area of your life or perhaps for guidance about your overall growth as a "whole" person.

Consider travel tours or cruises that include lectures and field-study experiences in addition to the fun recreational activities.

Educational researchers have known for decades that learning is one of the greatest "highs" any person can experience. When we cease learning, we start shriveling as people. Life and relationships become boring.

Choose to keep your mind and spirit alive and to apply what you learn to keep your life on an upward track. Invest in yourself. When you stop learning, you stop growing.

BOLSTER YOUR RESOLVE TO DO YOUR BEST AND SUCCEED

It has always been something of a mystery to me that people nearly always want to succeed personally, but at the same time, some people don't seem to want *other* people to succeed. It is as if we think there's only so much success to go around. This perspective seems to extend to include money, accomplishment, and even God's blessings. We seem to think that there's only so much money in the world, and only so much accomplishment. We seem to regard blessing as something that is in limited supply, even though we acknowledge that all blessing comes from an unlimited God.

If a person holds to this perspective that many of the best things of life are in limited supply, then it is a logical extension that a person must compete for his share. Sometimes that competition is fierce, and so are the feelings of jealousy that often go along with a competitive spirit.

In truth, there is no limit to the amount of success, blessings, money, or accomplishment in this world. Infinite God has both the capacity and the ability to provide infinitely. Every person in the world can be the best at what he or she does in a particular area of endeavor or knowledge. Every person can have wealth. The amount of money and material prosperity in the world is linked to the production of goods and services, and there's no end to the capacity for producing quality goods and services. In truth, the amount of money and material prosperity in the world is vastly more today than it has ever been. Every person can accomplish the goals that are related to life purpose.

There is no limit to the amount of success, blessings, money, or accomplishment in this world.

Why, then, do we perceive these unlimited "good things" are in limited supply?

Because not everybody has pursued life with equal passion, ability, steadfastness, obedience to God, or faith in God, which has resulted in the "good things" of life seeming to have been distributed unevenly. Too many people don't try... don't endure... or simply don't believe it is possible to attain what they desire. Others feel entitled, but don't want to work or exert effort—they want what others have and they seek to undermine and acquire what others have earned in ways that are unfair and sometimes illegal.

What can we do?

We can and must bolster our own personal resolve to succeed.

Not long ago, I met a woman whose husband and children had all turned against her. Whether their initial response was rooted in justifiable cause or not, their ongoing hatred of this woman was not justified. I asked this woman how she was handling their hurtful comments and rejection. She replied, "I decided I'm going to outlive all of them and I'm going to live well and for God."

I like her attitude.

There are two questions that only you can answer for yourself about your own future. The degree to which you have full resolve in your answer is the degree to which you will experience success.

Question #1: Do You Truly Want Increase?

Take a long, hard look at what you believe, and decide whether you believe it is possible for you to experience increase.

In talking about increase, I'm not talking about a windfall. Lots of people will tell you that they want more money. Lots of people want a life of fame and fortune. Most of them hope that it may be possible, but they truly don't think they will be "lucky" enough or have enough "breaks" to make it to the top. That's not a realistic decision about increase. That's pie-in-the-sky wishful thinking.

Ask yourself, "Do I want 30 percent more income?" Or pick any other percentage you like. Do you truly want an incrementally better life than the one you have right now?

A friend of mine told me about a conversation she had with a woman who is a multimillionaire. This woman had been working as a teacher. She wanted increase in her life so she could provide private art and music lessons for her children. Someone approached her with a part-time sales opportunity that gave her good cause to think that she could earn four hundred dollars a month by working two nights a week. She hoped to do even better than that, but the extra four hundred dollars a month was just what she needed at that time to accomplish her goals. Her husband agreed to watch their children on Tuesday and Wednesday nights and she pursued the opportunity.

Not only did she make the goal of four hundred dollars a month, but she began to inspire others to do what she was doing and she built a little business, which soon became a bigger business. She kept believing for greater and greater increase. Within three years, she was making enough money in her business to quit her teaching job and devote herself full-time to growing her new enterprise. It continued to grow until her once part-time job became a very large business that not only provided college for her children but enabled her to establish a foundation to give scholarships to many other children—both for art and music lessons, and for college.

Not every person who says she wants increase truly wants it enough to work for it, to wait for it to endure, and to press through the obstacles standing in the way of obtaining it.

Do not allow your present circumstances to lead you to a conclusion that increase is impossible. Increase is always possible to those who believe for it, and who are willing to invest themselves fully in the pursuit of it. I advise you to carefully examine *why* (motives) and *what* you truly want and desire. Sometimes people get what they want, but are disappointed with what they get.

Increase is always possible to those who believe for it, and who are willing to invest themselves fully in the pursuit of it.

Question #2: Do You Have Courage to Compete and Win?

The pursuit of all increase requires a degree of courage—are you truly willing to subject yourself to what other people are going to say?

Let me assure you, you will have competitors. No matter what form of enterprise or dream you pursue as the path toward increase, there are already people on that path. They *will* compete with you, some in a healthy, righteous way and some in a hateful, vengeful manner. There will be some who attempt to undercut you, buy you out, thwart your efforts, tarnish your reputation, or drive you out of business. They will seek to woo away your customers, clients, or members using all kinds of legitimate and illegitimate means. The higher you rise in success and profile, the more intense the competition is likely to become.

Are you willing to stick to what you know and pursue what you believe regardless of the competition and adversity you may face?

Consider those young people in their early teens or even childhood years who are pursuing a dream of Olympic medals. They know they are going to face competition—lots of it! Does this scare them? Perhaps a little. Does it deter them? Not the ones who will make it to the Games, and eventually to the podiums set aside for the winners.

When I was young I competed in gymnastics at a fairly high level of competition. Did I hate my competitors? No. Did I know they were training just as hard as I was? Yes. Did they drive me away from competition? No, they made me train all the harder.

If you are going to pursue increase, you must have the courage to face the daily competitiveness of life. Take on the challenge. Go for the win. Simply make sure it is what you really do desire. There is a lot that goes along with increase. To whom much is given, much is required (see Luke 12:48).

IT REALLY IS ALL ABOUT YOU...AND GOD

You may be reluctant to fully embrace your wonderful self because you think this makes you selfish or self-centered. That is not at all the case!

Your life really is all about you...and God.

I never advise any person to think that their life is all about themselves. But I do counsel every person to see their life as being uniquely theirs to embrace.

You were not created by God in order to be defined by another person.

You were not created by God so that you could become defined by a role or job or position.

You were created and fashioned by God so that He might fully define you and so you might discover His definition and fully embrace it for yourself.

Nobody can fully validate you...but you.

Nobody can dream your dreams, pursue your destiny, or receive the desires of your heart...but you.

Nobody can dream your dreams, pursue your destiny, or receive the desires of your heart... but you.

Nobody can pursue all of the resources necessary to achieve and accomplish something greater in your life than you've ever known...but you.

Nobody can bolster their own attitudes to pursue success...but you.

God has made you with a plan and imparted His presence and power to you. Together with God you can do *all* He has designed for you to do. You can be *all* He created you to be. You can have *all* that is necessary for the fulfillment of your purpose in this life.

Embrace what is, and you will be in position to embrace what is coming. As you prepare yourself today, you send opportunity notice to find you tomorrow.

MOVING ON

What might you be good at doing, apart from
what you are already doing?

MOVING UP

How big is your dream for your future?
Do you believe increase is possible for you?
How will you pursue it?

14

The Makeover You Really Want

Patti couldn't quit crying. Literally.

She had been going through a tremendous time of transition and change. Her husband had left her for reasons that didn't make any sense but which were set in stone nonetheless. Both of her children had gone away to college—one after two years of junior college, the other straight from high school. And she was facing the prospect of returning in a few months to the job market. She had spent the last fifteen years raising her children at home and pursuing volunteer activities at her church and in her community. She made three major life decisions.

First, she decided that since she had to move from the family home, she'd downsize into a new condo unit in a community fifty miles away. She felt that should give her sufficient space from her former husband, and at the same time, give her ample opportunity for retaining friendships.

Second, she decided to take a short course to update her computer and secretarial skills. And third, she decided to get an eye-lift to help her look a little younger. She thought that might help her in landing a better executive-secretary job.

The move to the condo and the short course had gone amazingly well. She loved her new home and discovered at school that she was still highly marketable and far more qualified than many women half her age.

The cosmetic surgery had gone terribly wrong. Something had happened that impacted her tear ducts and she couldn't quit crying.

"I wasn't crying all that much before," she told her aunt. "I was sad the marriage had ended, but I was happy about being out from under his constant infidelity and the stress of trying to uphold a happy outer appearance even as I struggled with embarrassment and shame. Now, I'm crying all the time and don't want to!"

Her aunt tried to make her smile. "Well, if people ask, just tell them they are tears of joy!"

Eventually, and after a second surgical procedure from a different cosmetic surgeon, Patti's condition improved and she quit crying. If anybody mentions eyelifts to her, however, she is quick to advise, "Get a fourth opinion! I'll give you my opinion. You need at least two medical opinions. And above all, get God's opinion!"

That's not a bad approach if you are facing any major decision during a time of transition or trial (or moving on and up). Find someone who has been there and get their advice. Seek out the experts. And above all, get God's opinion.

Find someone who has been there and get their advice.
Seek out the experts. And above all, get God's opinion.

Patti's story is one to which countless people can relate. We all desire renewal. We want to be updated, revitalized, reenergized, and transformed in positive ways. We want a makeover that allows us to put our best self into the spotlight.

Not long ago I was sorting through some information and promotional brochures for various "dream" centers as I began to lay the groundwork for a life-empowerment center I feel God is leading me to establish. Two words had been in my spirit and mind that I kept coming across: transformation and renewal.

I don't think I had ever fully realized before this time just how much we each crave a "makeover" in some area of our lives. Every person, it seems, has some flaw she would like to see transformed into greater beauty, some failure she would like to see transformed into a greater success, or some area of her life she would like to see transformed into greater purpose. Some people might even voice a desire for "an extreme total life makeover!"

Even if we don't desire a radical transformation, we often have a desire for rejuvenation — to be replenished and renewed in the areas life has depleted us.

We get tired.

We get discouraged.

We begin to feel a little frayed around the edges, overly stressed, or increasingly unsure about what we are to do or how we are to respond to our complicated world. It is the "wear and tear" of life and its responsibilities.

We want to feel refreshed, reinvigorated, and, at times, reinvented.

We want a renewed body, mind, and spirit.

God's Word has a great deal to say about both transformation and renewal. In fact, these seem to be two of the foremost "process" words in God's Word. One of the experts on these two words was the apostle Paul.

FACTORS THAT PRODUCE A TRANSFORMED, RENEWED LIFE

Transformation, simply defined, is a change from one state to another state of being. You may have seen the toys called Transformers that have been popular with children for years. With a few twists, what appears to be a robot turns into a creature, or vice versa. Generally, a life transformation involves changes that are far more significant and long-standing, and that are rarely reversible.

Perhaps the most complete physical transformation that any of us—and all of us—have experienced was our transformation from being a fetus to being a baby. We each have gone from living in a gravity-free watery environment in which we were free-floating creatures who received free nourishment, had no voice and no sight and no sense of smell, and had limited hearing…to living in a gravity-intense earth-and-air environment in which we had to learn how to become mobile, learn how to nourish ourselves, learn how to use our eyes, learn how to talk, and learn how to distinguish sounds and smells clearly and accurately. The change was fairly abrupt, no doubt uncomfortable at its outset (although no person can fully remember those first moments), and long-standing. Once birthed, we could not return to our mother's womb. The transformation was irreversible. We lost at our birth all capacity to live under water without an artificial oxygen source.

There is a degree of learning involved in all transformation. Some of that learning occurs immediately, some over time. The apostle Paul called upon those who were the first Christians to be transformed spiritually by the "renewing of the mind" (see Rom. 12:2). Paul went on to say that the renewed mind is a mind that is capable of knowing what is good, acceptable, and perfect or mature in God's eyes. These three words are vital to your understanding of God's processing of you in any time of transition or change.

There is a degree of learning involved in all transformation. Some of that learning occurs immediately, some over time.

Knowing What Is Good

God desires that you be able to tell good from evil. This may seem like a simple order, one easily accomplished. For many people, however, the lines are blurry between good and evil.

Countless people in our world today did not grow up in homes where good and evil were taught or lived out clearly. They had no role models for good. They saw no contrast between good and evil. People who grew up fifty years ago seem to have had far more real heroes and real villains in their world. And if they did not have good role models drawn from the news stories of their day, they certainly saw good guys wearing white hats and bad guys wearing black hats on their black-and-white television sets.

Consider the programs that children see today. Consider the lyrics of the songs they hear. Consider the books and magazines and comic books readily made available. It's very difficult to tell heroes from villains, and very hard to justify why certain behavior is truly wrong or right. Is the portrayed behavior wrong but seemingly for justifiable reasons? Does a good end seem to justify bad means? Does the portrayed "right behavior" result in painful situations that one would normally seek to avoid?

We who are "mature," or more perfected or complete, assume that every person has a built-in ability to discern good from evil, but there are many who often have very little ability to discern right from wrong. Evaluations about good and evil are often based upon the way a person "feels"—and feelings are subject to fads and whims. Emotions can put even the most rational person on a roller-coaster ride.

I have often said, "Your history tells you a lot about your destiny." Your personal journey in life offers insight and often effectiveness to minister and relate to others. My "journey" has given me the wonderful privilege to reach out and help others who have faced similar situations.

Through the years I have dealt with a number of women who grew up in broken homes, often with absent fathers, or in neighborhoods that were marked by poverty, gangs, very little regard for education, welfare checks for subsistence, immoral behavior and illegitimate children, extensive use of drugs and alcohol, and abuse of all kinds—mental, physical, sexual, verbal. In such environments, values become highly skewed. There are no "good guys"—there are only rich guys, poor guys, and some degree of bad guys. In such a world, "not quite so bad" can be interpreted as "pretty good!"

True good and evil are defined as good and evil according to standards that are fixed and agreed upon. The only sure standard for good and evil is found in God's Word. It is there that we find the fixed, absolute definitions for what is good behavior and what is bad behavior. Many people need to learn for the first time what those standards are. Other people need to relearn what they first learned as children at their grandmother's or mama's knee.

Why does God require that we learn good from evil? Because His master design for our lives is that we produce good.

When God looked at every aspect of His initial creation, He responded, "It is good." When God looked at the design for your life, He said, "It is good." God has designed you for good—for your good success, and so that He might use you to impact your world for good. You can't have good or do good unless you know what good is!

The second reason God desires for you to know good from evil is so you can make ongoing choices in your life for good, and so you can recognize evil and avoid it and the pain its consequences carry or make choices to turn away from it.

God placed Adam and Eve in the Garden of Eden and told them

*Recognize evil and avoid it and the pain
its consequences carry or make choices to
turn away from it.*

that they could eat of every tree and plant in the garden except the tree of the "knowledge of good and evil." Was God being mean or demeaning to mankind in this command? Not at all. It wasn't that God wanted to keep Adam and Eve ignorant or exempt of good. He walked and talked with them every evening, fully explaining all things to them and freely sharing with them all the good aspects of creation and how to enjoy every aspect of their life to the fullest. God did not want Adam and Eve to have a knowledge of *evil*.

The enemy came to Eve in the form of a serpent and tempted her with a lie: "You won't die as God said if you know good from evil. You simply will be as smart as God—that's why He said not to touch or eat that fruit. Surely you want to be smart, don't you?" Eve bought into the deception and lie and bit into the fruit and then gave it to Adam for lunch. He knew what he was eating, and ate anyway.

As a result, Adam and Eve were banished from the garden. Not only had they disobeyed God's only "thou shalt not" command, but the consequences of doing so meant they would be forever locked into an existence marred by evil. As it was, they were sent out into the broader earth with a free will to choose between good and evil—with a clear understanding of the consequences associated with both. They were given an opportunity to choose good, and in doing what God said was good, to put themselves into a position to qualify for entrance into a heavenly paradise one day—a world that was totally good and without any taint of evil. (See Genesis 2–3 for the entire story of Adam and Eve and the garden.)

What does that have to do with us today?

God's Word is our only reliable, millennia-proven source of definitions for what is eternally good for mankind and what is eternally evil. We must know God's commandments, or as my rabbi friend taught me, His habits, so we can say yes to them and adopt them into our lives and live according to them. We must know God's laws so we can say no to evil whenever we encounter it.

Having a knowledge of right from wrong, and good from evil, is basic to justice. We cannot seek to create a better world unless we have a good understanding of how that world might function — according to what standards, with what consequences.

Your purpose is ultimately to be an agent for good on this earth and to fulfill your purpose; therefore you need to be thoroughly renewed in your thinking so that you can make quick, decisive, and accurate decisions about what is good. The Bible is your resource in order to do so.

Knowing God's *Acceptable* Will

The renewal of your mind also involves knowing what is acceptable. This word *acceptable* refers to far more than knowing which fork to use at a formal dinner party, or knowing when something is being given to you as a finger bowl for cleansing your hands or as a dip for enhancing your food.

We need to know what is *acceptable to God*. Acceptability has to do with establishing or enforcing what is good in a particular time and place, for a particular people, and for a particular result. Acceptability has to do with timing and methodology. It is always directly related to the end results that God desires to establish.

There are many things that are *good* to do, but if you do those things in the wrong way, through the wrong channels, or at the wrong time, you can create havoc, disaster, or, at the bare minimum, embarrassment.

Furthermore, just because something is good to do does not necessarily mean that God has designed it for *you* to do. I can hammer a nail into the wall with my shoe, but that is not why my shoe was created and it is not the best means for hammering a nail. I can ruin a good shoe this way!

We are all commanded to love God with all our heart, mind, and strength. We do this by obeying the commandments in His Word. There are no justifications or "outs" for obedience to His commandments. They bring His life and goodness to us.

We are all commanded to love other people as we love ourselves. This means we are commanded to love ourselves as God loves us, and then love others as God loves them. Anything that detracts, subtracts, or invades another person's ability to achieve their God-given purpose on this earth is a transgression against that person, and missing the mark in God's eyes.

---

*We are all commanded to love other
people as we love ourselves.*

Knowing what is *good* to do is not nearly as difficult as knowing what is *acceptable* to do. To know what is acceptable we must ask God questions such as these:

- Are You asking me to take on this responsibility or commitment?
- What are the boundaries, parameters, and definitions related to what You are asking me to do?

- What are the end results that You desire for me to achieve? How will I know that I have succeeded in Your eyes?
- Are there prerequisites or first steps I need to take before I am ready to take on this big-goal assignment?
- Are You asking me to do this right now, or at some later time?
- How am I to do this? What method or methods am I to use? Is there a technology I am to employ? Is there a particular communication strategy I should use?
- What do I need to put into place in order for this to function smoothly, efficiently, and effectively? Is this a long-standing, permanent thing I am to establish and lead, or is it something I am to start and pass off to someone else?
- Is it something I am to do alone, or with others? If I am to do this with others, with whom am I to do this? How am I to make choices regarding those people?

In the end, "acceptable" is what God says is acceptable to you, and for your purpose to be fulfilled. You need to get precise instructions about what God desires, and then obey what He says. Your instructions cannot be forced upon others as their instruction.

The Bible tells us that if we ask and keep on asking, God will give us the answers we seek (see Matt. 7:7). He does not play hide and seek with us. He reveals to us what we need to know, when we need to know it, in order to enact His will.

Knowing God's *Perfect* Will

The word *perfect* in the Bible refers to wholeness. It refers to something functioning without friction or resistance—the image is one of a perfectly round ball rolling down a smooth-sided hill.

Wholeness in an individual produces balance and feelings of vitality and well-being. A person's spirit, mind, emotions, and body function as they were created to function, with an easy flow of energy and maximum strength.

Wholeness in an individual produces balance and feelings of vitality and well-being.

Wholeness in relationships between people is also marked by balance and harmony. A "whole" relationship is characterized by the Hebrew word *shalom*, which is often translated "peace" (Judg. 6:24 NLT). It is a relationship in which both persons are fully whole in their own identities, but also function together in harmony. They work together efficiently and without friction. They communicate easily and fully. They appreciate each other and value each other in ways that produce an atmosphere of acceptance and mutual respect. Wholeness in relationships is marked by mutual feelings of submission—giving preference to others in matters of methodology and style, and regarding others as worthy and as having dignity, regardless of their sex, social standing, financial worth, culture, or race. They deal with one another financially and materially in ways that are honest and productive.

The questions every person can and should ask about any given opportunity, job, career path, choice of spouse, investment, or any other major choice or decision are these:

Will this contribute to my personal wholeness? Is there anything about the opportunity or decision before you that can lead to spiritual error, physical disease, emotional turmoil, mental confusion, or overall imbalance and disharmony in your life? What about the opportunity will add to your well-being and wholeness?

What will the opportunity contribute to you spiritually, mentally, emotionally, or physically?

Will this contribute to the wholeness of others I value and love? Will this contribute to the overall spiritual, emotional, mental, or physical well-being of your family? Will it contribute to peace in your relationships with your spouse or children? Will it require any moral compromise? Will it produce anything that puts your family, neighborhood, or church in harm's way or subjects them to greater liability or loss? Will it promote greater communication and understanding? Will it produce results that are good for all involved, to the detriment of no person—not only now, but down the line?

If you can answer yes to these two questions, then there is only one more question to ask God: "Is this the *best*?"

Many things are good, some things are acceptable, and few things are "perfect" or contributing to wholeness—in the end, only one path is best for you.

Keep in mind, too, that wholeness is not something a person steps into like a new pair of trousers. Wholeness requires ongoing spiritual perception and a willingness to be corrected, refashioned, and renewed as time passes.

Even tires that are perfectly balanced on a car need occasional rebalancing as the car travels uneven roads or encounters jarring obstacles, curbs, and speed bumps. So, too, with our lives. We must continually seek God's good, acceptable, and perfect will. We must continually ask questions about all we undertake, and ask those questions with an open heart to discerning what is God's absolute best plan for our personal wholeness, the wholeness of others around us, and His purposes in our lives.

It is as we acquire an understanding of what is good, acceptable, and perfect before God that we are transformed and renewed. We begin to think differently. Our perspectives change. Our values adjust and come into alignment with God's values. Our understanding of truth comes into focus. Our knowledge of God's ways becomes clearer. Our hearts begin to beat in rhythm with God's heart of compassion and forgiveness.

We become new creatures. And as such, we become qualified for a new way of living and new areas of responsibility. We no longer function in reaction to the way the world says we should function. We function according to God's directives, and we become more useful to Him, accomplishing His purpose in the earth. In the end, we become prepared for the position and purpose He has already prepared for us.

THE ONGOING AND DAILY PROCESS OF RENEWAL

These questions I have posed about what is good, acceptable, and perfect pertain to things that exist in this material world, as well as to things of the spiritual realm.

Several years ago, I embarked on a focused and diligent health regimen to develop maximum energy and strength. I realized that life is a gift and it is my responsibility to value and protect my health. As part of that discipline in my life, I began to ask about everything I ate or drank, "Is this going to make me healthier, or will it detract from my health in the long run?"

---

*Is this going to make me healthier, or will it detract
from my health in the long run?*

I began to ask about exercise, "Is this going to make me healthier? Are there other forms of exercise that I need to do to create greater wholeness, more energy, and increased strength and stamina?"

I began to ask about my use of time, "Is this producing greater wholeness in my life?" There are times when I tend to work in excess and throw off the equilibrium God desires us to maintain as part of a balanced life. Part of being whole is having sufficient time for recreation and relaxation. I needed to make some adjustments to allow for genuine "down" time in my life, including sounder and longer hours of sleep.

I reviewed again the use of all my material resources, asking, "Does this contribute to wholeness—now and in the future? Am I building a legacy that benefits others? Am I in alignment with my core beliefs that financial prosperity is primarily for the purpose of affecting others' destinies?" I made adjustments in some of the ways I felt would better this mission.

I began to ask about various relationships, "Is this part of God's plan for my life? Is this relationship rooted in wholeness?"

I questioned every aspect of my life. I knew God's commandments. The issues of "good" were not in question. I also knew that my life's purpose was clear and in focus. I had few questions about what was "acceptable." But in every area, I questioned closely, "Is this perfect?" I evaluated things against the standard of *wholeness*. I asked God continually, "Is this the *best*?" The reality is, that is often a difficult question to confront yourself with.

I learned a tremendous amount over a several-year period. I encountered dozens of areas in my life in which I had settled for "okay" but not "best." I began to pursue *best* with my whole heart. As I did so, I saw certain priorities shift, certain areas of my personality became softer, certain areas that others might have considered weak became stronger. I realized one day, *I am being renewed!* There was a new quickness to my step, a new vitality that I felt upon awakening each morning, and a deeper sense of resolve and commitment than I had ever felt. I knew I was living more in alignment with my authentic self.

The process of renewal was not a concept—it was becoming a reality in my life. And it was wonderful! I was definitely moving on *and* up!

It remains wonderful, because the truth is, a process of renewal can be ongoing and unending. I don't expect God's renewal in my life ever to stop.

Just because one form of exercise, for example, is best during one season of life doesn't necessarily mean it will be best in the near or distant future. Just because one way of eating might be best while I'm traveling in the United States does not mean that those same food choices will be best for me if I am traveling in the Orient. Just because one designated bedtime is best for me when I am at home does not mean that it is the best bedtime for me when I am the speaker of an evening conference. These are small examples for an important principle to be applied in all areas of our lives.

The discernment of God's best is an ongoing discernment. We must place our lives before the Lord daily, weekly, periodically, and ask God the tough question: "Am I doing what is perfect—contributing to my wholeness and the wholeness of others—in Your eyes?"

A life of ongoing renewal is a life of continual examination. Nobody can do that work of personal examination but you.

USE GRIT TO CREATE A PEARL

I find it very helpful at times to remind myself that every beautiful pearl begins as a piece of grit. Most of us feel that way at times—as if we are just a lump of earth—and indeed, in our natural bodies, we are just that. God delights, however, in coating the grit of our lives with His beauty. The coating occurs as we deal with tragedies, trials, and troubles. Just as an oyster deals with rough-edged grit by coating it in a way that it no longer has jagged, tearing edges, so God enables us to deal with the troubles that come into our lives so that those troubles no longer tear at our souls or rip away at our peace.

Every beautiful pearl begins as a piece of grit.

God desires to transform even your memories of old painful experiences. He does not want you to experience raw pain every time you think of an old hurt. Rather, He desires that you have an ability to remember previous experiences and regard them as almost clinical examples of what to do, what not to do, and as shining trophies of what God can and will do if we trust Him.

You can never fully forget a previous time of trouble, just as you cannot completely ignore a current time of trouble, no matter how much you try to deny it or outrun it. God's provision for you is not the ability to forget completely your old wounding experiences, but to see them from a new perspective.

God desires that we learn.

God desires that we grow and change and develop.

God desires that we come to the place where we can look back and give Him thanks and praise for bringing us all the way through a tragedy or time of difficulty.

God desires that we use the grit that comes into our lives to produce pearls—big, beautiful, lustrous pearls.

MOVING ON

Are you confident that everything you are doing in your life is
both good and acceptable in God's eyes?

MOVING UP

What more might you do to discover and attain wholeness?
What might you do to discover and attain God's best?

15

Don't Ask "Why?" Ask "How?"

Vera is one of the most practical women I know. I found it hard to believe that she once considered herself to be a woman who had her "head in the clouds," with her feet not quite touching the ground.

"I was a philosophy major," she told me.

"Really?" I said. Frankly, I was astounded.

"That's right!" she said with a twinkle in her eyes. "Lots and lots of ideas."

"What happened?" I said, quickly adding, "You don't seem like the philosopher type."

"Oh, in some ways I still am," she said. "I still am concerned about the overall why of my life and I ask why as I read my Bible. But I'm not all that concerned about manmade philosophy. The first big change happened for me when I graduated from college. I quickly discovered that there wasn't a big market for philosophers. I became a computer programmer. If it didn't work, nobody cared about the philosophy behind the programs I was writing."

"I guess that would make a difference," I said.

"That wasn't all," she added. "I got married to an engineer—a no-nonsense guy who didn't care *why* things worked nearly as much as he cared whether they worked reliably and consistently every time. And then we had triplets. You have to be highly organized and very practical if you are going to feed, diaper, and raise triplets on any kind of schedule. After a while, I didn't really care what Plato or Aristotle had to say about life. I just needed to know where to buy diapers at midnight for the cheapest possible price. I stopped asking what and why, and started asking how, when, and where!"

Vera knows a great deal about transition, trials, and change—about moving on and up. She considers the foremost secret to her successful transformations to be this: she learned to ask, "How?"

Many times we can know the truth of what to do, but we lack information about how to apply that specific truth to our specific set of circumstances. We remain stuck, or immobile. We don't know how to get our lives off dead center. This seems to be especially true if we are experiencing a trial that is filled with emotional pain.

VITAL PRACTICES FOR MOVING UP

This chapter is about "how." If you have been knocked for a loop and find yourself in a painful time of transition, or paralyzed from past pain, or "stuck in a rut," there are five things that you absolutely must do if you want to regain your balance and strength sooner rather than later—if you want to move on and up.

Vital Life Practice #1: Begin to Voice Gratitude

When things are bad, it is a natural tendency to focus on what is in need of fixing. Before long, a preoccupation with what is bad can lead a person to conclude that everything in their life is bad and in need of fixing. If that happens, then everything will become bleaker and bleaker, and the person may lose all ability to sort out where to begin in making improvements, bringing healing to sickness, or forging reconciliation.

Gratitude is the cure.

You must never lose sight of what is right in your life.

You must continue to voice your thanksgiving for what you have. That is the only way to balance out your awareness of what you do not have.

You must continue to voice your thanksgiving for what you have. That is the only way to balance out your awareness of what you do not have.

And trust me, you have more reason for thanksgiving and gratitude than you have reason for complaint.

If you are alive to face another day, then be thankful you are alive!

Be thankful for every bit of health, strength, and energy you have.

If you can read these words, then be grateful for your mind and your ability to think, dream, analyze, reason, decide, choose, set goals, make plans, and take in new information.

If you have food in your cupboard and a source of clean water to drink, be grateful.

If you have a roof over your head and clothes to put on your body, be grateful.

If you have a friend or anybody in your life who genuinely loves you, be grateful.

The list is unending!

Gratitude isn't just a nice idea. More and more scientific research into this area is proving that an attitude of gratitude bears significant good results when it comes to both physical and emotional healing, career advancement, marriage satisfaction, successful parenting, the development of a prosperous life, the accomplishment of goals, and the "likeability factor" necessary for developing and maintaining meaningful friendships.

Gratitude puts the focus on what is working or beneficial in your life, and it leads you to pursue ways in which the good things in your life might become better. Almost as a by-product, the negative aspects of life slough away or improve.

It isn't enough just to "think thankful thoughts." Voice your thanks. Make statements of gratitude the foundation of your prayer life. Be quick to thank others around you for their help or their ongoing contributions of love and support to your life. Be quick to write thank-you notes to those who give to you of their time and treasure.

God's Word is filled with admonitions to give thanks to God for all of life. At no time, however, are we told in God's Word to thank God *for* all things that happen to us. We are commanded, rather, to give thanks to God *in* all circumstances. We are only able to do that if our spirit is ruling over our emotions and minds. If we look at what God is doing, has done, and is capable of doing on our behalf, we have countless reasons for offering verbal thanksgiving to God. If we look at circumstances alone, we can quickly become discouraged. Keep your mind and heart, therefore, on who God is and what God promises. Ultimately, this will prevail.

Keep your mind and heart on
who God is and what God promises.

Vital Life Practice #2: HALT before Things Go Too Far

One of the cornerstone concepts in many therapeutic practices is the concept embodied by the acronym HALT (Hungry, Angry, Lonely, Tired). We are wise to recognize and put a stop to certain trends, patterns, or behaviors in our lives as soon as we discern them. HALT is used as a reminder to stop the action if you are hungry, angry, lonely, or tired. These are emotional circumstances that often generate poor decisions with undesired consequences. Therefore, it is better to "halt" the action and refuse to proceed if you have allowed yourself to become too hungry, too angry, too lonely, or too tired:

Too hungry. Being too hungry can lead to bad food choices that give a quick energy fix but produce a huge feeling of exhaustion later. This "low" can fan the flames of discouragement and depression, as well as decrease the mental abilities related to concentration and memory. In addition, allowing yourself to become too hungry can put into motion factors that lead to blood-sugar problems, especially hypoglycemia and diabetes. Choose instead to eat small balanced meals throughout a day—complete with protein and complex carbohydrates found in fresh fruits, vegetables, and whole grains. Your body will thank you, but so will your mind and emotions.

Too angry. If you feel yourself becoming angry, take action. Go out for a brisk walk. Engage your mind in something other than the problem that is related to your anger. Refuse to vent your anger at a person or animal, or to destroy property. Turn your anger into a positive action that can benefit you and others around you. Let your anger find a place of purpose to manifest itself. Get busy and clean out that closet. Go out and weed the garden. Go to your workshop or studio and make something. Take up a cause and use anger in a healthy way to motivate you.

Too lonely. If you allow yourself to become too lonely, you will only be locked into your own problems. You can be alone and not be lonely. However, when that feeling of isolation, which is different from solitude, comes to you, decide to do something about it. Call a friend. Make a date for lunch. Sit outside on your porch and strike up a conversation with neighbors who might be out for a walk after dinner. Go to a reputable coffee shop and strike up a conversation with another person. Go to a nursing home and talk with a person who has few visitors. Or best of all, get to a Bible study or church service!

Your contact with other people can help you realize anew that everybody has troubles and pain, and most people have a good handle on how to compensate or resolve their troubles and pain. You have to be around people to learn from them. You have to make yourself available to *be* a friend if you want to *have* a friend. Get outside of yourself and give of yourself.

Too tired. Don't allow yourself to get overly tired. Eating correctly and exercising regularly can help you sleep better. Make sure you get sufficient rest at night. Learn how to put yourself to sleep without the use of pills. There are entire books now on the subject of sleep. If you don't know how to sleep, or think you don't need sleep—get informed. You do need sleep and there are many helpful things you can do to ensure that you get sufficient sleep. Sleep is God's method for restoring the tissues and organs of your body, and for bringing closure to things in your mind so that you can be more creative and see solutions to life's problems with greater clarity.

Too much hunger added to too much anger, added to too much loneliness, added to too much "tired" can create a downward spiral that very quickly leads to depression and despair, and at times, to highly addictive behaviors that are very tough to reverse.

Recognize the warning signs in your own life and take action.

Vital Life Practice #3: Get Wise Counsel

Regardless of what type of problem you are facing in your life, there's somebody who knows *something* about how to turn that problem into a solution. Find that person or seek out that information.

Seek out wise counselors. That means seeking out someone who believes in God, and more specifically, someone who believes in the power and desire of God to heal, restore, and bless.

Seek out wise counselors.

A wise counselor is also someone who knows answers that can be directly applied to your problem. Not every counselor can give wise counsel about every topic.

If you need marriage or relationship counseling, go to someone who has wisdom in regard to relationships.

If you need financial counseling, go to a financial counselor.

If you need counseling about your physical health, go to a physician, nutritionist, or qualified trainer or fitness expert. The point is to get the wisdom where it can be found.

God's Word tells us that there is benefit in a "multitude" of counselors (Prov. 11:14). Don't just listen to one person. Get a second opinion—or seek out a second voice to confirm or corroborate the advice you are given.

Always check the counsel you are given against God's Word.

And, at all times, recognize that counsel has both value and limitations.

I am a firm believer in the value of good counsel. It can be a tremendous benefit if a person truly wants to grow and change.

Counseling is of little benefit to a person who doesn't want wise counsel, or who doesn't want genuine change and growth.

Some people are so entrenched in their I-am-right-and-you-are-wrong position that they will not even attempt to see another person's point of view, or they are so in need of being "100 percent right" that they are unwilling to negotiate or change. Still others are so ill—mentally, emotionally, or spiritually—that they truly need a divine act of personal healing before they can begin to address the problems they might have in a relationship. There must be an honest approach of identifying where a person is and what they are ready to receive.

Vital Life Practice #4: Recognize the Limitations of Compromise

Not all problems can be resolved by talking about them.

In some cases, talk is just that...talk.

Talk is best when it produces real change of behavior, and unless agreed-upon changes result in agreed-upon behaviors, talk fails.

Your will cannot override the will of another person.

You cannot make someone love you or accept you—and neither can all of the wise words of a counselor impact the will, respect, love, or acceptance of another person.

You can only examine your own heart and motives, and seek to change and grow in ways that you know are truly God's will for you.

There are times when another person demands something that is outside the parameters of what God commands. We are never to compromise if another person asks us to participate in behavior that crosses lines of personal convictions, rebellion, or disobedience—insofar as we are capable of opting out of their choices and behavior. We are never to compromise what we know to be God's plan and purpose for our own lives.

There are also times when another person demands something of you that you simply cannot become or do. It is not a part of the way God has created you.

There are also times when another person demands something of you that you simply cannot become or do. It is not a part of the way God has created you.

For example, some people have a huge capacity for love. If their spouse has a small capacity for love, the two people will be mismatched. Even if the small-capacity spouse gives all his love, he cannot fill the "love container" of his spouse. No amount of cajoling, demanding, crying, or pleading can result in a person giving more than the person is capable of giving.

"But," you may be saying, "my spouse isn't even trying to give his love to me." That may be true, but it also may be true that he is trying his best and his best is not what will satisfy you. You may need others in your life to pour love into you in ways that are appropriate and moral. Again, this is with the recognition that only God can truly fulfill and satisfy you.

Some people have a huge amount of energy for work and accomplishing tasks. If their spouse has a small amount of energy, the two people are mismatched and will need to accommodate this difference in each other. There's no point in railing at the low-energy spouse to do more and be "less lazy." The person is simply incapable of expending more energy. On the other hand, the low-energy spouse can plead all she wants that her spouse must "stop working around the clock" or continue to work even when he pretends to be relaxing. Her words will fall on deaf ears. He cannot throttle back his basic energy level. Two people who are mismatched in this way are going to have to find a way to compensate for their differences.

Some people have tremendous creative energy and their minds never seem to rest. Other people are more concrete, with very little ability to think conceptually or creatively. There's no point in berating each other for these differences in thinking wavelength. Two people who have these differences are going to need to find a way of accommodating their different approaches to problem solving and choice making.

Are such compromises—or as I like to say, negotiations— possible? Yes. But only if both people are willing to do so in a way that is mutually satisfactory.

I recently heard about a fifty-year-old man who has attention-deficit disorder. Though he has had this condition all his life, he just received this diagnosis two years ago. Suddenly much of his life makes sense to him. His behavior also suddenly makes sense to his spouse. They realized that they had intuitively adjusted to each other in ways that made it possible for them to have a happy marriage and family life. But learning about this disorder also led them to learn even more ways of compensating for their differences. They discovered ways to accommodate each other that have made their relationship even more satisfying.

They were both willing to make changes and to learn and grow in their relationship skills, even after more than twenty-five years of marriage.

I recently heard about a man who had been involved in pastoral marriage counseling with his wife for more than fifty years. He said in a lecture about pastoral counseling that the most common thread he and his wife had been able to discern about marriages that worked was this: both people wanted to remain married more than one person wanted to leave the marriage. That is his view from the years of his experience.

Having worked with many people on a variety of levels, I have learned that if one person wants out of a relationship, that person will find a way out.

Very often, nothing the other party can do will matter. The decision to part ways may be delayed, but unless there's a true change of heart in the person who wants out, the marriage will eventually dissolve.

Am I gloomy about marriage? Not at all. Quite the contrary.

Do I believe that good, committed, happy, and long-standing marriages are possible and God's design? Absolutely!

I'm saying this to affirm to you that if you and someone you love—perhaps a spouse, a child, or even a friend—have been in a relationship that has ended or have been to a counselor for years and there's little progress, don't beat yourself up over the failure of that relationship. There are many dynamics to maintaining a committed relationship. Because the relationship is over does not mean you are finished. I know it can feel that way at times, but God has a future for you. He knew *all* things from the beginning. He is able to heal every place you have been hurt and every place you have brought hurt. God is a repairer of the wounded soul. When all attempts have been made for the relationship to stay together and it still ends, then recognize the areas of personal responsibility and allow God to bring development and growth to you. Seek God's forgiveness, seek forgiveness from each other, and agree to part in peace.

If you truly forgive and seek to live in peace, you may find that God will weave your lives back together down the line, but don't

God is a repairer of the wounded soul.

sit down and wait for that to happen. It is just as likely *not* to happen as to happen. By seeking God's forgiveness and forgiving each other—and agreeing to part in peace—you at least can walk away with the satisfaction that you have done all you knew to do, and you can leave the consequences to God.

Vital Life Practice #5: Find Someone Who Needs What You Have to Give

When we are in pain or are going through a troublesome time of transition, we very often conclude that we have nothing to give. We feel weak, without sufficient resources, depleted of ideas, and wrapped up in solving problems. The truth is, the best way to work through a transition time is to begin to give out of your pain.

There's always *somebody* who needs *something* you have to give.

It may be your time...perhaps even just a listening ear.

It may be a loaf of your homemade bread...or the gift of garments that are no longer your size.

It may be a volunteering of your services at a shelter for the homeless...or going to a nursing home to visit someone who has no regular visitors.

It may be reading to a child in an impoverished after-school program...or volunteering as a teacher's aide in a public school.

It may be befriending a child who is in foster care...or coaching a Little League team.

You have talents and abilities that are worthy of sharing. Get out there and start giving!

The more generous you are in your giving, the more you are likely to discover new opportunities to give. In the process, you are likely to make new friends and acquire helpful advice. You are also likely to discover more about the purposes God has for you in the next phase or at the next level of your life. And you are definitely moving up as well as moving on.

MOVING ON

Do you know how to make the changes
you believe you must make?

MOVING UP

To whom might you give as an act of your faith as you
undergo God's transformation processing?

16

Face Your "Issues"

From Jody's perspective, the issues were very clear. Her husband had promised her that he would never become like his father, and shortly after their wedding, she discovered that he had become exactly like his father! His father was a lazy man, unable to keep a job and unwilling to put out any extra effort to help his wife around the house. His father refused to learn new skills to make himself more marketable. His father refused to go to church, calling it a "crutch." Like father, like son, Jody thought.

Jody went to a counselor seeking advice about how she might encourage her husband, and if she couldn't encourage him to return to being the more ambitious, more responsible, and more spiritual man she had dated, she needed advice about how she might cope with his behavior.

Instead of getting the practical answers she sought, she found herself being asked questions about her own upbringing, her own relationship with her father, and about other men who had influenced her concepts related to marriage. She said with a very big sigh, "I never thought of myself as having issues!"

We have come to adopt that word "issues" for things we may once have termed "difficulties," "inner turmoil," "suppressed pain," or "dysfunction." By whatever name, issues are perceived as obstacles to us and we intuitively know that they are better dealt with than ignored—especially if we want to move up as well as move on.

Issues are perceived as obstacles
to us and we intuitively know that they are better
dealt with than ignored — especially if we want
to move up as well as move on.

Generally speaking, issues are rooted in long-lasting areas of pain or emotional injury. We develop issues because we have been unable at some point in our past to experience healing of emotional rejection, criticism, abuse, or behaviors that represented anger, prejudice, injustice, or hatred to us.

DON'T LET OLD ISSUES DICTATE YOUR FUTURE

The issues of our lives come in many packages. Some of those packages seem to have no expiration date!

God's Word tells a story about a woman who had an "issue of blood" for twelve years. This was a literal, physical issue, but it was a condition that also had serious emotional consequences. Because this woman was hemorrhaging, she was considered to be "unclean" by others in her society and therefore was shunned. She was banished from religious ceremonies and if she went out in public, she was required to cry out, "Unclean, unclean!" so that people could stay far away from her. She was an untouchable, and no doubt was lonely beyond our imagination. Her physical issue led her to have emotional issues.

This is often the case—the way we perceive ourselves physically, or the physical ailments we have, can isolate us from friendship and love. The reverse is also true. The emotional issues we have can physically keep us apart from other people, or even cause certain physical ailments.

We are wise to admit that we have issues.

We are even wiser to take action to resolve and heal them.

One day this woman who had an issue of blood for twelve years ignored the cultural and religious customs associated with her condition and she pushed her way through a crowd of people to reach down and touch the hem of the prayer shawl being worn by Jesus. In doing so, she touched Jesus in His spirit. And in doing that, her activated faith tapped into Jesus' divine desire and ability to heal. She was instantly cured (see Mark 5:25–34).

When I speak about this incident, I often say, "She linked herself to the Word in faith." Jesus was and is the Word of God, the living human fullness of God's message to mankind, eternally God and yet fully human. This woman with an issue found her answer in the Word. She tied it to her life by her faith. And the result was a complete physical healing and a full restoration to normal life as a woman in a small city in ancient Israel.

I believe the same thing happens when a person today ties his or her life to God's Word in faith. The powerful truth of God's Word overcomes all issues, if we will only believe that it can and does. We must *believe* to the point where we *behave* as if God's Word is already accomplished in our lives. We must declare to our innermost soul that the Word of God will rule over any lie, accusation, or issue that appears to have a grip on us.

---

*We must **believe** to the point where we **behave** as if God's Word is already accomplished in our lives.*

Face up to the possibility that the issues of your life may be ruling you, just as the "issue" in this woman's life ruled her daily routines and behaviors. The bruises on your face and body may be keeping you from going to an appointment that could advance your position. The fear you feel deep within may be holding you back from speaking up, even though the opportune moment has come for you to take a stand. The prejudice you have experienced for decades may have led you to slump your shoulders in despair—your low feelings of self-value may be keeping you from holding up your head and walking tall as you go for a new job interview. Feelings of being unworthy because you did not complete high school may be at the root of your refusing to accept a social invitation.

I can't begin to anticipate all the issues of your life, or all the ways in which they are limiting you, but I know that countless people today are trapped in isolation and loneliness because of something in their lives that they believe is better kept secret. They can be surrounded by many people and still be alone.

The only definitive cure I know for those issues is the Word of God applied to life with faith.

FAITH OVERCOMES ALL ISSUES

Faith is believing that what God says in His Word is the only opinion that counts. Faith is believing that life *can* change, in good and beneficial ways. Faith is believing that God will be faithful to His Word and that what He has promised for one, He has promised for all. Faith is what leads us to go against the tide of our issues and take a bold step toward seeing those issues resolved. Faith is what leads us to believe with confidence that all issues are subject to healing and restoration.

In pushing her way to Jesus, this woman with an issue of blood faced the distinct possibility that she would be found out. Even after she felt healing power flow into her body and Jesus asked, "Who touched me?" she tried to remain silent. It was with "fearing and trembling" that she finally fell on her face before Jesus and admitted that she had touched the hem of His prayer shawl (Mark 5:33).

In many cases, the greatest obstacle a person faces is not the issue of their life but fear that their issue will be discovered by others. There is a saying in the mental-health world that a person can never be mentally or emotionally healthier than his or her secrets. It is what we keep in secret that keeps us sick. It is what we expose to the light of truth and God's power that leads to our healing.

Jesus did not criticize this woman for her sickness. Neither did He criticize her for her deception or for touching His garments while she was unclean. He looked beyond her condition and locked on to her faith.

God does the same in dealing with us. He does not hold us in contempt or ridicule us for either our condition or our failure in not coming to Him sooner. He looks at our faith in the present moment and latches on to it in order to pour into us His healing that gives us courage for our future.

One of my favorite psalms is Psalm 27, a portion of which says:

The LORD is my light and my salvation; whom shall I fear? The LORD is the strength of my life; of whom shall I be afraid? . . .

Hear, O LORD, when I cry with my voice: have mercy also upon me, and answer me.

When thou saidst, Seek ye my face; my heart said unto thee, Thy face, LORD, will I seek. . . .

I had fainted, unless I had believed to see the goodness of the LORD in the land of the living.

Wait on the LORD: be of good courage, and he shall strengthen thine heart: wait, I say, on the LORD. (vv. 1,7–8, 13–14)

ACCEPT THE RESPONSIBILITY THAT IS YOURS

Accept the responsibility that *you* are the one who has the greatest opportunity to build a life that is going to be rewarding, pleasurable, and fulfilling to you.

Accept the responsibility that you *are the one who has the greatest opportunity to build a life that is going to be rewarding, pleasurable, and fulfilling to you.*

I have lived for years in Florida where hurricanes are common. I have seen firsthand how people have dealt with extensive storm damage. There are some who sit down, wait for help, and often refuse to do very little on their own. They hope someone will come along to restore life for them, with very little effort on their part. Some of those who have moved into government housing in the aftermath of a storm that occurred many years ago are still in that government housing waiting for government assistance.

Now I certainly am not decrying our need to help one another, and at times, government assistance may be just the short-term help that is necessary for a person to regain their emotional and material footing. But I am also certain that the government can never do for a person what a person can do for himself. Those who have chosen to work hard and rebuild their homes and their lives in the aftermath of a storm are nearly always those who emerge from the storm experience stronger and with something that is even better than what they lost. Their relationships with other family members, friends, and fellow church members are nearly always stronger too. In many cases, the new homes and businesses they have built are better constructed, more beautiful, and more satisfying to them than the old homes and places of business they lost.

If you are waiting for someone to come along and supernaturally solve your problem with snap-of-the-fingers speed, I have bad news for you. It isn't likely to happen! You live in a state of existence by waiting on something or someone to give you life. Existence is what you find; life is what you create.

Yes, God can and does supernaturally heal people in an instant. But it is the person's responsibility even in those cases to rebuild their bodies for ongoing strength and healing. One of the men I admire a great deal experienced a devastating illness when he was a teenager. He was taken to an evangelistic service where a preacher prayed for him and he experienced a dramatic healing. He remained weak, however, even though the disease that had been ravishing his body was cured. His mother said to him, "You should lie down in the afternoons and take a nap to get your strength back. But don't take off your clothes and crawl back into the bed. Lie on top of the covers with your clothes on."

What difference did that make? His mother explained, "If you crawl back under the covers you are going to think of yourself as being sick again. You will take on the same mind-set you had when you were in that bed dying from disease. But if you stay on top of the covers with your clothes on, you are going to have a mind-set that you are just taking a little nap to gain more strength."

How you think about your life has tremendous impact on the responsibility you are willing to take for your life. If you believe you can recover fully, and even produce or experience something better than you have known in the past, you are going to set your mind toward accomplishing that higher goal. On the other hand, if you do not believe you can do anything to recover, or that others must do that work for you, you are likely to go nowhere. You will remain in the miserable mudhole in which you currently find yourself. Instead, create the life you desire and are destined to live out by the grace of God.

TAKE RESPONSIBILITY FOR YOUR SINS AND ERRORS

If there is any part of your current trouble that is related to your personal sin or error, accept the responsibility for your own actions. Confess your faults to God, and ask for His forgiveness. God's Word tells us with assurance that if we confess our sins to God, He *will* forgive us (see 1 John 1:9).

Confess your faults to God, and ask for His forgiveness. God's Word tells us with assurance that if we confess our sins to God, He **will** *forgive us.*

I know from years of driving at night in central Florida that a person's windshield can become so splattered with bugs that seeing out the windshield is nearly impossible. If I get my eyes on the mess made by the bugs, I lose focus on the road ahead.

This happens in life. We are the ones responsible for driving our own lives down the road God has put us on to accomplish His purposes. We need to keep our eyes on the road and refuse to let others tell us where to turn, what to do, how fast to go, or how to drive. At the same time, we must keep our focus on what lies ahead, not on the messes that come to cloud our vision.

The only solution for a bug-splattered windshield in central Florida is to pull off the road at the next gas station and wash the windshield. In life, when our vision becomes obscured by the messes we encounter or even produce, the only solution is to come apart before the Lord, repent of our errors or our lack of vision, and ask God to cleanse us and renew in us a clear sense of who we are and what He has planned for us. True repentance involves a change of direction. It is embracing God fully and letting go of all that is causing you to "miss the mark."

LET GO OF WHAT YOU WERE NEVER AUTHORIZED TO CONTROL

Many of the issues people often confront as they "face themselves" fall into the category of control issues. They are either feeling controlled by another person, or they are being told they are controlling.

The bottom line is this: you ultimately cannot govern the actions, attitudes, or words of another person. And another person cannot control you unless you allow it.

Certainly there are those who try to manipulate, coerce, or exert so-called power plays over other people. We tend to call them abusers, dictators, or warlords. In the end, the things they rule with an iron fist crumble. A desire for freedom and self-determination nearly always rises up, sometimes in a matter of months, sometimes not for several centuries.

In our personal lives, most of us do our best to avoid those who manipulate, coerce, or seek to control us with strong shows of force. We do not want others to determine the details of our lives or put a lid on our potential. In like manner, nobody wants you to do that in return.

What you can do is seek to influence others to behave in positive and loving ways, including positive and loving behavior toward you. We influence others in two primary ways—first, we influence others by the way we treat them. And second, we influence others by the way we treat ourselves.

It is very difficult to dislike a person who speaks well of you, does good things for you, encourages you, and prays for you. On numerous occasions, I have witnessed the hardened heart of a person become softer in the face of acts and words spoken in kindness by the very person once perceived as an enemy.

It is very difficult to continue to rail against a person who won't fight back. It is difficult to oppose a person who is generous toward you and who speaks well of you in public.

You can greatly influence others by what you do, if at the same time, you refuse to be influenced by their rejection or ridicule.

You will also have great influence as you treat yourself in the manner you would like to be treated by others, regardless of how they are presently treating you. You don't need to argue or even speak in your own defense. You simply need to value and respect your own self in the ways you want others to value and respect you.

If you dress, speak, and act in a way that shows you respect yourself, your culture, your faith, and your abilities...other people will respect you.

If you dress, speak, and act in a way that shows you respect yourself, your culture, your faith, and your abilities . . . other people will respect you.

If you treat yourself with kindness, refuse to demand the impossible from yourself, give yourself sufficient time for reflection, and forgive yourself for your own failures...other people will treat you kindly and forgive you for your flaws and failures.

If you are humble but confident in your own abilities...other people will value your abilities and listen to what you say.

In contrast, if you disrespect yourself—perhaps abusing your own body or failing to care for your own cleanliness and appearance...other people will disrespect you.

If you constantly belittle or ridicule yourself...other people will be more prone to devalue you.

If you are proud and arrogant...other people will look for ways to avoid you or discount what you say.

We are quick to want God to process other people around us—to change them, to cause them to grow—so they will do the right things and everything can be put right. We are quick to want what we believe will result in our continuing to live the life we are presently living, only better.

God rarely does that. Rather, He changes *us*. He causes us to grow and change. He calls us to move into a new landscape where our lives may be very different than anything we ever envisioned.

LEARN GOD'S WORD FOR "LETTING GO"

Issues often arise because we do not know when to hang on and when to let go. We don't know when to "hold 'em" and when to "fold 'em." In some cases, a person may want to let go but doesn't know how.

God has a word for "letting go." That word is *forgiveness*. Forgiving is an act of releasing a painful memory or the guilt connected to a past sin—yours or a sin someone else has committed against you. It is letting go.

Forgiveness is not a matter of saying that something didn't hurt or wasn't important. That's denial or dismissal.

Forgiveness is not a matter of giving up any claim to justice. Rather, it is trusting God to exact His justice.

Forgiveness is saying, "I no longer will hold on to this pain. I give it to God. I let it go."

When we forgive, we open our hands and place the hurt that we have been clutching into the much bigger hands of God. Then, with our hands empty before Him, we allow God to put back into our hands what He desires. God takes our crumpled-up, tear-stained, blood-dripping, filthy rags of sin—and all of the shards of memory, shame, and guilt associated with our darkest hours. He hands back to us a new opportunity that is fresh, clean, pure, and good.

Sometimes the number-one person God requires us to forgive is the person who looks back at us from our own mirror.

LEARN TO LET GO OF YOUR OWN PAST

Your future is the time that *will* come to pass in God's timing and according to God's methods and processes. Your past doesn't determine your outcome. The future God has designed for you is your outcome.

God never binds you to your past. The apostle Paul knew this clearly. He wrote to the Christian church he established in Philippi: "This one thing I do, forgetting those things which are behind, and reaching forth unto those things which are before, I press toward the mark for the prize of the high calling of God in Christ Jesus" (Phil. 3:13–14). To "press" means to resist that which would resist you. In other words, you decide to not let anything hold you to your past, but with a determined resolution you reach for your tomorrow.

The future God has designed for you is your outcome.
God never binds you to your past.

Paul did not act in the present tense of his life according to his past. He certainly knew and did not deny the previous ways in which he had persecuted Christians. He certainly remembered all of the hardships he had experienced for the sake of spreading the gospel across the Gentile world—everything from beatings to shipwrecks to imprisonments to times of intense personal, physical, and emotional suffering. But Paul did not drive toward his future with his eyes on the rearview mirror of his life. He did not dwell on the negative things he had experienced, nor did he dwell on his previous accomplishments. Paul said that he chose to forget all things that were in his past.

THE IMPORTANCE OF FORGETTING

Forgetting is something you can will yourself to do. Forgetting is a choice you can make. Choosing to forget does not mean that we deny something happened—or that we refuse to admit that we once acted in a certain way. Rather, forgetting is saying, "I choose not to rehearse this memory in my mind. I choose to let the past lie in the past. I refuse to allow the past to predict my future."

Forgetting is saying to our own self, "I will not devote any portion of my memory to that painful event or that hurtful conversation or action. I am freeing up all of the 'memory' on the hard drive of my brain's computer for storage of new information and the processing of new experiences. I choose to dwell on the goodness of my future."

Certainly, your past may inform your present choices or actions—we certainly should learn from past mistakes so we don't repeat them. We certainly should remember to the best of our ability what has worked well for us in the past, and what hasn't worked at all, so that we can optimize our decisions and put our emphasis on what is beneficial, productive, and effective. We err greatly, however, when we believe that what we have done in the past has predictive power over our future. If God does not judge you according to your past, who is man to do so? Never allow man's opinion to override God's judgment in your life.

Just because you failed in your last relationship does not mean you will automatically fail in your next one—as long as you learned the reasons for your past mistakes and made adjustments in the way you relate to other people.

Just because you failed in your last business venture or job does not mean you will fail in your next one—as long as you learned the reasons for your past mistakes and have made adjustments.

Just because you have been single for the past four decades does not mean that you will or should be single for the next four. On the positive side, just because you won the last golf tournament or hit a home run the last time you came to bat does not mean that you will win the next golf tournament or hit a home run in your next at bat. Just because you won the Miss Beautiful contest twenty years ago does not mean people today will reward you the same for your appearance.

Every opportunity you encounter in life should be approached as a blank slate—it is a chance for you to do your best, to put into effect everything you have learned, and to trust God for all consequences and outcomes. Every day is a new day. Embrace it as such.

In many ways, forgetting is closely linked with forgiving. Many

Every opportunity you encounter in life should be approached as a blank slate.

people say, "Oh, I can forgive, but I can't forget." The question to ask is, "Why are you so intent on remembering?" What do we gain from hanging on to hurtful insults or ridicule, recalling words of rejection or alienation, or revisiting memories of hate-filled, prejudicial, or abusive behavior we once experienced? Why not let go? Why cling to the pain when God offers healing and renewal?

The act of forgetting is this: choose to think about something else! Choose to focus on the good and positive. If a painful memory comes to mind, choose to direct your attention to something at hand that requires your full concentration. Engage your mind fully in a new body of information, a problem, a conversation, or anything else that requires you to think actively.

If there's something you need to forget, in all likelihood there's something God wants you to learn. There's something you need to acquire intellectually to fill the mental space that is presently being occupied by what it is you need to stop thinking about! Ask God what that new area of study might be.

REACHING FORWARD

Read again what Paul wrote to the Philippians. Note that he said he was "reaching forth unto those things which are before." Reaching implies a diligent attempt to lay hold of something that is just barely out of one's grasp. Reaching involves a conscious and intentional use of the entire body. When a person reaches for something, there is no flailing of arms in hopes of making contact with something. A reach is aimed or focused, stretching toward a particular object.

In order to reach for something, you must have in mind what it is you are hoping to lay hold of.

People have told me they want to be rich...but they have no clue what kind of work they want to do in order to earn the kind of money they want to have.

A reach is aimed or focused, stretching toward a particular object.

People have told me they can hardly wait to be married, settle down, and have children...but they cannot give me a description of the character qualities they desire in a future spouse, define for me what "settle down" means, or give me a godly reason for wanting to have children.

People have told me they think it would be wonderful to be famous...but when I ask, "Famous for what?" they don't have an answer.

The sad reality is that the vast majority of people seem to go from day to day, just taking what comes their way, going with the flow, and feeling "lucky" if something a little good happens or if nothing truly bad happens. They do not live authentic lives from the inside out. They do not have a clear sense of direction for their lives, nor can they succinctly state what they believe to be their purpose on this earth. Even those who have some sense of their own worth and abilities often cannot state clearly what kind of legacy they hope to leave to this world. It would be a shame to die and never have lived.

How are you going to know when you have attained what is going to be truly fulfilling or meaningful to you?

If you are simply grasping in the dark for whatever you might find, how will you know that what you grasp is God's best? Don't waste another moment wandering, but focus in to find what has already been established for you in the plan of God.

Paul was enthusiastic about his future. He was eager for it. That wouldn't have been the case if he had not believed wholeheartedly that his future was going to be more glorious than anything he had known thus far. It is important to recognize this: Enthusiasm rooted in your own self-inflated emotions can be easily deflated. Real enthusiasm is found in faith. When you build a life or dream in God or in spirit, the natural by-product is enthusiasm.

What about you? Are you leaning toward what is next for you? Are you eager for it? Can you hardly wait for the dawn of tomorrow to see what good things God has for you?

THE CHALLENGE OF PRESSING

Finally, note this phrase from the apostle Paul's letter to the Philippians: "I press toward the mark for the prize." To press is to exert, to push, to expend energy and effort. It means to move against all opposing forces, to overcome all things that create inertia, and to strip away all things that cause friction. Again, to resist that which would resist you.

Nothing of value falls from heaven into our laps. God desires to give to us *all* things that are for our benefit. But the windows of heaven are opened to us only as we do—with our whole heart, mind, strength, and soul—those things that God has instructed us to do. There must be application to instruction in order to see results.

Obedience to God's commands and principles takes intention and effort. We do not automatically obey. Obedience is learned. It is restrained and thoughtful—not impulsive and reactive. In the vast majority of instances, our spur-of-the-moment spontaneous behaviors in response to circumstances around us are rarely what we would do if we gave serious, objective forethought to our actions. Our spontaneous behaviors are much more likely to be foolish, random, emotionally reactive acts that rise from self-centered, immoral, greedy drives and lusts.

---

*Obedience to God's commands and principles
takes intention and effort.*

Obedience to God's principles involves a reining-in of our personal out-of-alignment desires and a concerted effort to consider and enact what God desires. Obedience demands that we do what God says, regardless of how we feel. It demands that we discipline our lives, which is accomplished by reliance and yielding to the Holy Spirit.

The kind of "pressing" that Paul describes bears a quality of consistency. It is not a "spurting" of effort, but a steady, continual pressing. It is that kind of strength and pressure that eventually wears down all obstacles and opposition. It is that kind of pressure that breaks through barriers.

What is the motivating force for us to develop disciplined obedience and consistency of effort? It is the prize that God has for us.

THE PRIZE

The good news about God's prize program is that He has a different prize for every person. That means each of you can be a winner by being true to yourself and being the best *you* God has called you to be!

Paul specifically said that the prize toward which he pressed was the "high calling of God in Christ Jesus." The calling of God on His life was unique — nobody else was called to do what Paul was called to do. But the good news is that nobody else is called to do what *you* are called to do. God determines the specific calling for each of us.

The encouraging and motivating joy in all this is that you get to win the best and highest prize just by being 100 percent *yourself*, in 100 percent service to God! If you are willing to serve God to the best of your ability in the area where He has placed you, you can and will win the prize He has designated just for you.

Keep in mind these two attributes connected with all genuine prizes:

A Prize Is Valuable

A material prize may be fairly inexpensive materially, but the intrinsic value can often be beyond measure. For example, the metal in an Oscar statue is worth only a few hundred dollars, but the value of having received an Oscar from the Academy of Motion Picture Arts and Sciences can mean millions. The stem of laurel leaves awarded to Olympic winners in ancient Greece could be purchased in an open marketplace for a few pennies. But having that wreath placed upon one's head at the end of fierce athletic competition meant a prestigious invitation to move in the highest and most noble circles in Greece. It often opened the way for an influential position in the highest ranks of government or the military.

A Prize Is Lasting

The best prize is one you keep always. In the natural world of competition and politics, a person may not win the same contest next year or hold on to the office after the next election, but the fact that the person once won a prize stays as a part of that person's reputation and identity, and often the title associated with that prize becomes part of the way in which others address a person. Retired military generals are still addressed as "General." World-champion athletes still hold the honor of "champion" even decades after their victory.

In the spiritual realm, the prize we win is eternal. What a person gains as a prize from God is beyond measure in value. It becomes part of the person's identity forever.

What a person gains as a prize from God is beyond measure in value. It becomes part of the person's identity forever.

Do you know what you are pressing to receive?
What are you disciplining your life to achieve or attain?
What is demanding your steadfast, consistent effort and focus?
How, exactly, are you moving on and up?

MOVING ON

What are the issues that may be holding you back from experiencing positive change and renewal?

MOVING UP

Is there someone you need to forgive?
Is there something you need to forget?
Is there a new goal that you need to press forward to reach?

17

Dodging the Mudslinging

Marty wished there was another woman in town who had her same name. It might have given her a temporary breather. The sad fact was that she was guilty as charged.

She had kicked herself a hundred times for falling in love with her boss. She knew he was married. She knew he was about to run for public office. She knew his wife's family was wealthy. She knew deep inside that he would never leave his wife and marry her. She knew that she was violating God's commandments in starting an affair with him. She willfully walked into sin and she knew she had disappointed her church as well as herself, her family, and her friends.

Yes, she was sorry for what she had done.

Yes, she took full responsibility for her own actions.

Yes, she had repented and personally asked for forgiveness from both the man and his wife, and in a letter, she had asked forgiveness from his children.

Yes, she had repented before God—she had confessed her sin and knew she had been forgiven for it.

And then, one night she packed a suitcase and moved out of the country. Nobody has seen her or heard from her in two years, apart from an untraceable phone message that said, "Don't worry about me. I'm not coming back. I have taken a new name and a new identity. I want to build a new life."

There are no doubt many people who are going through times of emotional pain and trial who wish they could skip town like Marty did.

Have you ever opened a newspaper to find yourself being crucified in headlines?

Have you ever turned a page in a magazine to find inaccurate details about your private life there for the whole world to read?

I have had both experiences.

No matter how much I thought I would feel numb to false accusations or to the baring of my private life, I still felt pain.

There's a special type of pain that occurs once you know that the whole world has access to your private pain and brokenness.

WHEN PRIVATE PAIN BECOMES PUBLIC

The Israelites' King Saul and his sons Jonathan, Abinadab, and Malchishua died during their battle against the Philistines on Mount Gilboa. Throughout the Bible, mountains are regarded as places of ascendancy, power, and control. The deaths of Israel's leaders on Mount Gilboa was the beginning of a transition time—it was a place of death for the old regime, which would make way for the new regime of King David in the years that followed.

After Saul and his sons were killed, their bodies were hung publicly. The defeat was a stunning one, clearly visible.

The defeats and losses that are subjected to public scrutiny are generally no more painful, in actuality, than the ones people experience in the privacy of their own homes. But they are more humiliating. The pain of a divorce, tragic loss, or abuse is just as intense whether anybody knows about it or not, but when the public focuses its leering eyes onto that person's tragedy, the pain is layered with multitudes of embarrassment—even if the person is a totally innocent victim of what has happened. When the public becomes privy to and often misjudging of a person's private pain, that person faces an extra degree of difficulty as he transitions to what God has next. It is perhaps even more important for the person to shut himself away or be in a "safe place" of being restored for a period in order to regain his own confidence and sure footing.

The defeats and losses that are subjected to public scrutiny are generally no more painful, in actuality, than the ones people experience in the privacy of their own homes. But they are more humiliating.

When your personal tragedies hit the public stage, enemies seem to crawl out of their holes to take advantage of your pain.

Why does this happen?

No doubt it happens, at least in part, because when your detractors or enemies perceive that you are in pain, they perceive that you are in a weakened position and more vulnerable to attack. Predators always seek out the weakest animal in the herd or flock, not the strongest. Human predators seek out those they believe are easy targets, incapable of defending themselves or blind to the dangers around them. This has always been difficult for me to personally comprehend as I have "reached" for the wounded in life with the love of God and His "balm of Gilead" (see Jer. 8:22). Nevertheless, it is true.

No matter how weak you feel, or how much pain you are experiencing, stay alert. The painful stage of transition is a prime time for people to seek to take advantage of you—legally, financially, socially, materially, and in all other ways.

I have seen this happen countless times. A person who has

just experienced a major loss—perhaps death of a loved one or divorce—will suddenly be surrounded by people who will claim to be their friend, but in truth want to use the person's weakness for their own advancement. They will offer help, advice, or other seemingly beneficial things that, in the end, do not help the person advance.

The biggest danger is that you, in your weakened state, are likely to turn to these human "helpers" to give you what you truly need to receive directly from God. People may impart information to you, but only God can impart wisdom. People may seek to comfort you, but only God can heal your broken heart and give you a peace that far surpasses all human reasoning. People may offer assistance, but only God can strengthen you from the inside out.

Especially beware of those who operate with guile. Guile is treacherous. It is the ability to be cunning and clever in tricking or deceiving another person. The person who has guile will appear to be one thing, but in reality is the exact opposite. The Bible warns us to beware of wolves in sheep's clothing (see Matt. 7:15). When you are going through a painful transition, check out everything that is presented to you as being "true." Ask questions. Double-check facts and figures. Get a full accounting in writing. Make sure all terms are spelled out. Stay awake and stay alert not only to what is being said but also to what is being meant.

The Bible warns us to beware of wolves in sheep's clothing.

Personally stay innocent. Do not seek to hurt others or gain from others what is not rightfully yours. God's Word tells us to be "wise as serpents, and harmless as doves" (Matt. 10:16). To be harmless means to be innocent of trying to hurt others. At no time are we given license from God to strike first at our enemies or to take vengeance into our own hands. We may have to fight for what is rightfully ours or defend ourselves when attacked, but we are not to go out seeking a fight.

To be wise as a serpent means to avoid conflict whenever possible. A snake is smart in that it knows when to get out of harm's way. Snakes tend to coil and strike only when they are surprised. If given sufficient warning of impending danger, they will quickly slither away. As much as possible, learn to identify the signs of a "potential" fight and walk away before tempers flare or angry words are exchanged.

The apostle Paul wrote this advice to the early Christians in Rome: "If it be possible, as much as lieth in you, live peaceably with all men. Dearly beloved, avenge not yourselves" (Rom. 12:18–19). That is the way, Paul said, to ensure that you will not be overcome by evil, but will conquer evil with good (see Rom. 12:21).

Strength Heightens the Attacks

If your detractors and enemies at first perceive that you have been hit, but they don't see you crumble or collapse, they may very well choose to attack you with even greater boldness and vitriolic self-righteousness.

Do not be surprised if you suddenly find yourself dealing with enemies once you begin to walk boldly in the direction God places before you. People of diverse backgrounds will form coalitions against you to keep you from succeeding—these people may have very different reasons for confronting you, and they may not even like one another, but they nevertheless will join forces in an attempt to defeat you. You may be amazed, as I have been, at how quickly and fiercely such opposition can arise. Even so, recognize that no enemy forges weapons against you without that enemy first perceiving that you both have the capacity to and are likely to succeed, and that your success is for a good that will counteract their evil activity.

Truly successful and godly people are not threatened by other successful and godly people.

People who are truly intent upon producing good in this world are not threatened by the efforts of others who are focused on producing good.

It is people who are greedy, power hungry, or steeped in lust who move the quickest against positive, godly initiatives. It is people who are low in self-worth who perceive other people's success as detracting in some way from their own value. It is people who deal with their own evilness of heart who judge you as they are themselves. Remember, the heart is a filter. Whatever a person judges you with is what is in his heart.

I am not referring here to normal competition for the consumer dollar, sports championships, media ratings, or other forms of day-to-day competition. I am referring to all-out assaults that are intended to kill or destroy another person—perhaps not a physical death, but certainly a killing of reputation and a destroying of influence.

Sidestep the Trap of Vengeance

Even as we face those who seek to hurt us, or those who reject us, we must be very careful that we do not engage in vengeance. Vengeance is taking matters into your own hands to be prosecutor, judge, and jury on those whom we perceive to have injured us in some way. God's Word tells us that vengeance belongs to God—it is His responsibility (see Rom. 12:19). Our responsibility is to trust Him, release our enemies into His hands, and get out of the way. Try to remind yourself during these times of unjust persecution that oftentimes hurting people hurt people. That will help you to view their behavior with eyes of compassion. I believe that is one of the main reasons God said, "Vengeance is mine." Only God has the ability to really know the intent and motive of a person's heart.

God's Word tells us that vengeance belongs
to God — it is His responsibility.

The following is a composite of the stories so many women have told me:

> After my husband left me for a younger woman, I wanted God to destroy him and destroy their marriage. I could hardly bear the fact that God seemed to bless their marriage with a baby. I struggled with feelings of bitterness, anger, resentment, and hatred, although I kept telling myself and others around me that I had forgiven my former husband. Many times I wanted to take vengeance.
>
> Then the day came several years after my husband left me, when I saw him from a distance at a shopping mall. He was stooped over and using a cane. He looked as if he had aged thirty years. I discovered through friends that he had a terrible autoimmune disease, and also that his new wife had abandoned him when she learned he was ill. She had taken their little girl and was refusing to grant him unsupervised visitation rights, claiming he was abusive. I actually found myself feeling sorry for him, and although I certainly did not want him back in my life, I prayed God would help him.
>
> And then... the most amazing thing happened. My former

husband's new wife came to see me. She apologized to me with tears, saying that she was sorry she had believed my former husband's lies about me. She asked my forgiveness. I had an opportunity to tell her how God had helped me and provided for me. I encouraged her to trust God with her life.

If you had told me several years ago that this would happen, I never would have believed it. God has His ways!

Nobody can deal with your abusers, detractors, insulters, or enemies like God can deal with them. Trust Him to work in you, and in them. That does not mean we are to sit idly by on bleachers waiting for the games to begin—that would be a waste of your time. Get on with your life! Release the past to God.

I also want to encourage you that it is entirely acceptable to pray as the psalmist prayed: "O God, to whom vengeance belongs, shine forth!" (Ps. 94:1 NKJV). Ask God to act on your behalf and trust Him to handle your affairs.

Develop a Higher and Broader Perspective

Rather than spend any energy or concern with those who seek to diminish or destroy you, choose to develop a higher and broader perspective. First and foremost, know that God is using all things for your spiritual growth and development. He is conforming you into the image of His Son.

See the barricades that are thrust before you as a sign that the enemy of your soul is already anticipating your advancement.

See the assaults against you as a sign that God is about to increase you and enlarge your territory.

See that kiss of betrayal against you as a sign that God's purposes are being fulfilled in you.

See that trial of your faith as a sign that God is undertaking your perfection or maturity.

Why see obstacles, pain, pressure, and trouble in this light?

Because the enemy of your soul would not put up a barricade against you unless he recognized that God was moving you forward deeper into his territory. The enemy would not assault you if he did not think you were about to thwart his evil purposes. The enemy moves against you to stop you the more you allow God to do His work in you to advance you. Opposition is an opportunity for you.

God's Word tells us that when our faith is tested, God is working in us a process of perfection (see James 1:3–4). He doesn't "begin" every time. The enemy of your soul uses tests, troubles, and trials in an effort to destroy you. God uses these acts of the enemy to produce in you a stronger character capable of handling bigger blessings.

Recognize that the most potent weapon in the enemy's arsenal against you is fear. Your faith, however, has the capacity to be stronger than your fears...if you will activate your faith and release it into action.

Recognize that the most potent weapon in the enemy's arsenal against you is fear. Your faith, however, has the capacity to be stronger than your fears.

Remember, faith is the Word of God backed and authorized by God Himself. At times, the enemies of God seem to know the power of instilling fear more than the friends of God seem to know the power of releasing faith.

When Sennacherib put Israel under siege, he sent this message to the inhabitants of Jerusalem: "Whereon do ye trust, that ye abide in the siege in Jerusalem?" (2 Chron. 32:10). After deriding comments about King Hezekiah, Sennacherib went on to taunt the people, saying, "Know ye not what I and my fathers have done unto all the people of other lands? Were the gods of the nations of those lands any ways able to deliver their lands out of mine hand? . . . No god of any nation or kingdom was able to deliver his people out of mine hand, and out of the hand of my fathers; how much less shall your God deliver you out of mine hand?" (vv. 13–15).

Then God's Word tells us that Sennacherib wrote letters to people in the city, and he also sent his messengers to cry with a loud voice in the Jews' own language. The purpose of these messages was to "affright them, and to trouble them" so that Sennacherib might "take the city" (v. 18). Sennacherib knew that a people filled with fear is a people easily defeated. Fearful people have no will to fight because they have no hope of victory.

Fear always deals in weakness—both the weakness of the person and the weakness of God. Fear predicts failure and a negative outcome.

Faith always points toward strength—both the strength of the person and the strength of omnipotent God. Faith anticipates success and a positive outcome.

- Can you identify those things that are instilling fear in you today?
- Have you identified what it is that you are afraid will happen?

The Power of Resistance

God's Word tells of a vision given to the prophet Zechariah in which Zechariah saw Joshua, the high priest, standing before an angel of the Lord, and Satan standing at his right hand to "resist him" (Zech. 3:1).

This word "resist" means to accuse, hinder, repress, present a barrier, or put something in direct opposition. The end result of resistance is either breakthrough and forward motion or break-down and backward motion. You will allow your tribulation to either propel you to a new level of strength or stop you.

Part of processing is resisting the resistance mounted against you.

God's Word tells us that when we resist the devil, the enemy of our souls, he must flee. I believe the same is true for those inspired or controlled by the enemy of our souls. If you resist them in the spiritual realm—calling upon God for help and believing that He is your strong ally—your enemies will have no recourse but to back down. That isn't my prediction; that's God's promise (see James 4:7 and 1 Peter 5:8–9).

Refute Lies Spoken to You

You can waste a tremendous amount of time and energy seeking to address all lies and false accusations that are spoken about you. The same for combating rumors and innuendo. But when lies are spoken to you or in your presence, you do have an obligation to respond with the truth. Do not let another person plant a lie in your own memory bank. Immediately say to that person, "What you are saying is not true." If you read a lie about yourself in print or hear a lie about you in the media, immediately say aloud, "That is a lie from the father of all lies. I reject that lie." Don't passively accept a lie or false accusation into your own mind. Ultimately, it is what you say to yourself about yourself that matters the most.

> *Do not let another person plant a lie in your own memory bank. Immediately say to that person, "What you are saying is not true."*

Is there precedence for doing this in God's Word? Most definitely. When critics came to Jesus with lies, He immediately called the lies for what they were (see John 8:44). When He was led as a sheep to the slaughter and did not defend Himself against His accusers, it was in order for the purpose of God to be accomplished.

THE TRUTH ABOUT "HELPFUL" CRITICISM: IT USUALLY ISN'T!

People are quick to say that they are offering "helpful criticism." The two words very rarely belong together.

Criticism is usually levied against a person with an intent of exerting power over that person, and often it is intended to diminish another person in order to elevate self. As a result, most criticism hurts and is not the least bit helpful. Such criticism tends to focus on fairly minor flaws or one-time errors, yet the criticism is often couched in terms of "always" and "never." The critical person is likely to say, "You never take me anywhere" or "You always put me down in public"; when in truth, the person may have refused to go to an event *this* coming weekend or may have corrected misinformation in the presence of two close friends.

When you criticize another person's efforts or behaviors, you are voicing a demand that the other person change to conform to your standards. You set yourself up to be right, and the other person wrong. If you are on the receiving end of criticism, you know that even more than if you are on the giving end of criticism. When you are criticized, you feel "put down"—you feel inept, unqualified, unskilled, ignorant, or unrehearsed.

Not only is the critical person voicing a demand that others conform to his or her standards, but the critical person is setting himself up as a role model of excellent character—"more excellent" than the person being criticized. The person who receives such criticism feels not only unskilled at a task but unworthy of love.

What is the better approach?

Suggestion. *Helpful* goes with the word *suggestion* or the word *advice*. Suggestions give other people the option of taking advice or rejecting it. If a person feels empowered to make a choice, he nearly always will choose to accept good advice. Say to someone you want to influence, "May I make a suggestion?" or "I have a suggestion for you to consider."

Be concrete in what you advise. Be specific. Tie your suggestion to a particular behavior or way of doing something. Tie it to a specific result intended or a specific goal. Be very concrete in the way you believe a character trait might be manifested. Don't simply say to a person, "I suggest you find a way to be more joyful." Rather, make a suggestion about a very practical manifestation that reflects joy. "When you are feeling down, I suggest you find five things to praise God for."

Don't offer suggestions you haven't tried personally. There's little value to advise unless you personally know that it works.

"You might try," "You may want to check out this reference," and "You may want to consider" are all phrases that fall under the suggestion umbrella. And then add, "That worked for me and here's how."

When you are faced with verbal assaults under the label

"helpful criticism," tell the person criticizing you that his words are not helpful, and kindly ask the person to only "suggest" advice to you that is practical and that you can readily implement. If the person looks at you as if he doesn't know what you are talking about, hand him this book and ask him to read these pages about criticism.

Many critics think they are very clever and original. In reality, there are very few new approaches to criticism.

Critics rarely spend their time criticizing people who are mediocre. In a rather perverse way, criticism against you should be seen as a compliment. Critics only go after those they believe deserve to be taken down a peg or two from the pinnacle of their success.

Critics only go after those they believe deserve to be taken down a peg or two from the pinnacle of their success.

Most critics are motivated by their own jealousy or lack. They simply do not believe that you, of all people, deserve the position you are in or the increase you have experienced in your life.

I want to be your greatest cheerleader, encouraging you to believe that you *can* have a greater life and that you deserve it as much as anybody on the planet and that God has it for you!

Anticipate and Repel Your Critics' Attacks

We are always wise to anticipate verbal mudslinging from others. We each are responsible for determining that we will *not* allow false accusations, rumors, gossip, or intentional or unintentional lies about us to deter us from what we know to be our potential or our destiny.

The Bible has an amazing story along these lines.

After the Israelites were taken into Babylonian captivity, with the best and the brightest of Jerusalem hauled away to slavery in Babylon for seventy years, the city of Jerusalem fell into great disrepair. When news of the crumbling walls of Jerusalem reached Nehemiah—a servant in the court of the king of Persia—he was dismayed and he began to fast and pray that this situation in his homeland might be reversed. The Persian king was moved by Nehemiah's deep concern, and eventually the king not only sent Nehemiah to Jerusalem to repair the walls of the city but also funded the repair work.

When Nehemiah arrived on the scene, he discovered that the damage was extensive. He also discovered that there were those in the immediate area who did not want the walls of Jerusalem to be rebuilt. These adversaries were not people who would benefit from living inside a city with secure walls and gates. Rather, they were people who lived in outlying areas who perceived that the wall would hinder their ability to pillage the city.

The first thing Nehemiah's adversaries did was to mock him and those who worked to rebuild the wall. They attacked with words and ridicule, saying such things as, "What are these feeble Jews doing? Do they really think they can fortify themselves? Who do they think they are to attempt this?" (see Neh. 4:2). Their verbal mudslinging was not unlike the attacks you are likely to experience if you set a goal for good and begin to pursue it.

Five Areas of Verbal Attack

Critical verbal attacks tend to cluster in these five areas:

1. Critics will attack your character. Rather than attack your plan, your goal, or what you have already said or done, your critics are likely to resort to personal insults. They will "name call." Nehemiah's adversaries called the Jews "feeble." They labeled the Jews as weak and incapable, in hopes that the Jews would see themselves as so. If an enemy can get you to agree with him about your character flaws or inadequacies, he doesn't have to fight you with weaponry—he will have defeated you with discouragement!

You will not pursue excellence that you do not believe you deserve or can attain. If you internalize criticism about what you are incapable of doing, you will cease to give your best effort to your goals and plans, and you will fail.

Many of the negative labels we internalize are ones that would not stand up to extensive cross-examination or close scrutiny, but perhaps because we have heard them in our past or in our childhood, we tend to give them more weight than they deserve. If anyone has ever called you "stupid," "incompetent," "a weakling," "foolish," "inadequate," "unworthy," "unlovable," "strange," or any other negative personal attribute, you carry a memory of that insult with you. You are susceptible to any taunt or word of criticism that rekindles an old negative self-image or the pain of the old insult. Be aware of that tendency. If you are hit with a criticism related to your personhood or character, say aloud to yourself the truth of who you really are: You are lovable, capable, worthy, talented, gifted, intelligent, and strong! You are a child of God!

You are lovable, capable, worthy, talented, gifted, intelligent, and strong! You are a child of God!

Sometimes a personal insult is related to a person's race, nationality, body type, sex, or appearance. If you are ridiculed in any of these areas, absolutely refuse to internalize the insult! God created you! God uses and blesses people of all races, of all nationalities, of all body types, of both sexes, and regardless of appearance. Successful, wealthy, accomplished, talented, and famous people come in all shapes and sizes, all colors and backgrounds, and all degrees of beautiful and not-so-beautiful!

2. Critics will question your ability and determination. Nehemiah's adversaries questioned the Jews' ability to fortify themselves. The historical fact was that in the previous seventy years, the Jews had *not* fortified themselves. Their enemies reasoned, "If they could have done it, they would have done it." They leveled the criticism that the Jews were incapable or lacked the willpower to do the job of rebuilding the walls and restoring the city gates.

Just because you haven't done something already doesn't mean you can't, won't, or shouldn't do it.

An older friend of mine said recently, "I know that I'm not going to win a footrace in the Olympics. But that doesn't mean that I can't train for and complete a 15k run for a charitable cause."

Another friend told me, "I am too old to have another child, but not long ago, I met someone who worked for a faith-based adoption center and he told me about the tremendous need for adopting teenagers who are still hoping for a family and a home. I'm not too old to do that!"

It's never too late to study something you've always wanted to learn. It's not too late to develop a skill you've always wanted to acquire. It's not too late to develop the talent that has been silent in your life thus far. It's not too late to start your own business, get involved in a new type of ministry, or pursue a dream you've had since you were a child.

3. Critics will wonder if you will be willing to sacrifice in order to achieve what you want to accomplish. Nehemiah's adversaries asked, "Will they sacrifice?"

Critics will wonder if you will be willing to sacrifice in order to achieve what you want to accomplish.

Anything worth accomplishing has a cost associated with it. The cost may be in terms of money or resources, or it may be a cost in terms of effort, energy, and time. The cost may involve letting go of some long-standing affiliations in order to devote focused time, energy, effort, and resources on a new set of goals. Nearly always as a person pursues a major goal, he feels a loss of personal time and resources.

Are you willing to spend less time on the phone talking to friends, fewer hours walking the mall, less time on the golf course, or fewer hours sitting in front of a television set? Are you willing to cut back on some expenses in order to have more money to devote to building a new enterprise or pursuing a new project—fewer meals out, fewer new clothes and shoes, or less money spent on a favorite hobby?

Not long ago I heard about a young woman who decided that she really wanted to go on a short-term missions trip to Central America. She didn't have the money for the trip and she didn't want to ask anybody for money. She did ask a financially savvy friend to help her rethink her personal budget. The trip was nine months away so she had some time to adjust her expenses and also add to her income. She had been living in a rental property on her own and she took in two roommates to help share the expenses. She was able to carpool with one of them to work. She took on a part-time job on Saturdays, and also took on several house-sitting and pet-sitting jobs as they were offered to her. She gave private piano lessons to four children on Monday and Tuesday evenings. And she decided that she could take her own "designer coffee" with her from home rather than stop by the coffee kiosk where she had been buying a large latte every morning. She dropped several subscriptions to media services or publications. Not only did she have enough money for her missions trip to Central America, but she was able to put two hundred dollars in savings *and* help give a scholarship to a person who hadn't been able to save as much as she had.

At first, what this young woman did felt like a sacrifice. But her new patterns of living quickly became more pleasure than sacrifice. She discovered that she liked having a roommate and enjoyed teaching piano. The house-sitting and pet-sitting jobs gave her a sense of being "on vacation" from her own home, and by having roommates, she felt her house was secure even as she stayed overnight in other houses.

In most cases what we "sacrifice" in the pursuit of a new goal is short-term. And in many cases, it is a sacrifice of what is truly an "excess" or something unnecessary to our lives.

At other times, the sacrifice involves greater change.

Are you willing to move to a new city in order to take on the new job? Are you willing to move out of the old familiar neighborhood to a new neighborhood that offers better opportunity and a better school system for your children? Are you willing to go overseas to undertake the missions challenge that burns in your heart?

Are you willing to downsize your home or sell valuable possessions in order to have more to give away? Are you willing to give more of your free time to volunteer for a worthy organization? Are you willing to take a needy person into your life—and perhaps even into your home—even if it means an inconvenience to you?

Other people may say that you don't have what it takes to sacrifice in order to achieve a goal that is important to you. Their opinion isn't the opinion that counts. The *only* opinion that counts is yours.

4. Critics will mock or question your work ethic. Nehemiah's adversaries said, "Will they make an end in a day?" (Neh. 4:2). In other words, "Do they think they can finish this quickly?" The adversaries were questioning the Jews' work ethic and their ability to stay with the project until it was completed.

People will always question your "stick-to-it-iveness." They will always be looking at you slightly askance wondering if you really are serious about putting in the long hours over the long haul. Two of the most difficult things in life are starting something and finishing something.

I learned not long ago that a surprising number of all those who pursue Ph.D. programs never complete the coursework for the program, even though they may have enrolled in several semesters of study. Then, half of those who do complete the courses do not go on to write the dissertation that is required for them to earn the degree. That means that 75 percent of those who start and do some work toward a Ph.D. bail out at some point short of finishing the degree program.

These are smart people who have already earned a master's degree (so they know what advanced studies are like and they know the effort required), and they are people who have invested real dollars in paying real tuition bills. Even so, they give up.

The reality is that most people who start goals give up before they reach them. Some of them may be almost at the goal line when they bail out of the game.

We'll discuss perseverance and endurance further in another chapter, but let it suffice here to say: you must set yourself to reach your goal and refuse to be deterred by those who tell you that you do not have the "staying power" required to accomplish something of value. You alone determine how important your goal is to you, and how long you intend to pursue it.

You alone determine how important your goal is to you, and how long you intend to pursue it.

5. Critics will question your resources and resourcefulness.

Nehemiah's adversaries asked, "Will they revive the stones out of the heaps of the rubbish which are burned?" (Neh. 4:2). The adversaries did not believe the Jews had any worthy building materials. Neither did they think the Jews had the resourcefulness—the reasoning ability or creativity—to construct a wall and refashion strong gates. Neither did they understand the power and principle of restoration. God can take what others can "trash" and bring forth treasure.

Your detractors are likely to come at you with comments such as, "Where do you think you are going to get the money for that?" Or, "Do you know how much that is going to cost? It's impossible!"

Some may say, "Who do you think you are? No banker is going to trust you with a project like that! Given your track record, who is going to invest in your idea?"

Still others may say, "Don't you know you are a poor person and poor people don't do things like that? You are foolish to try to rise above your lot in life."

If you are seeking to accomplish something intellectually, or earn a degree of any kind, people may question your aptitude.

If you are seeking to do something of a spiritual or religious nature, people may question your spirituality or your spiritual maturity.

If you are seeking to do something that seems beyond your social standing or economic status, people are going to question your "worthiness" or your "acceptability" by those they see as belonging to a higher social class.

Get ready for the insults! Don't let the mud that your adversaries are slinging stick to you!

The truth is, there's *always* a way to learn more, do more, earn more, give more, and acquire more.

I recently heard about a young man who was labeled "learning disabled" when he was in elementary school. He barely made it through high school. Even so, he was determined to go to college. He asked for help in learning how to compensate for his learning difficulties and he discovered a way of studying and preparing for tests that helped him greatly. He took six years to complete four years of college but he graduated. Many of those from his neighborhood who had earned far better grades in high school did not complete college.

I also heard recently about a young woman who wanted to go to college but she did not have the grades for a scholarship. Her parents made too much money for her to receive low-income grants, but they were divorcing and neither parent was willing to help her (each parent insisting that it was the other parent's responsibility). All of her friends suggested she get a job and forget college—after all, that's what they were planning to do. Nobody thought of this young woman as being very creative or resourceful. After all, she had never worked even part-time during high school and she had never shown any great motivation to set goals and accomplish them.

She refused, however, to give up on her dream of being a college graduate. Her aunt invited her to live with her in a neighboring city where a good state college was located. She was grateful for this opportunity to be with a relative she loved and have free room and board. She quickly accepted her aunt's invitation. She took out a small student loan to make a down payment on her tuition bill and pay for her first semester's books, and then she got a full-time job from four in the afternoon to midnight. She went to classes in the morning and studied in the afternoons and early evenings. She made good enough grades after one year to qualify for a small scholarship, but she kept her job. She received a raise at work, which helped her pay off her student loan and pay cash for her tuition bills.

At the end of four years, this young woman graduated debt free from college. And after four years of work experience, the company where she had been working all those years gave her a big promotion with an excellent salary, benefits, and opportunities for advancement! Not only that, but a young man she had met in college also began to work for the same company. The year after they both graduated, they suddenly realized how much they loved and valued each other, and they married.

Don't let anybody tell you that you can't find the money you need to pursue your dream. There are all kinds of no-money-down opportunities in our world today. You may need to search long and hard for them, but they are there. There are all kinds of jobs available that can help you get your foot in the door of the career field you want to pursue.

> *Don't let anybody tell you that you can't find the money you need to pursue your dream.*

Deep in my heart, I had a knowing for years that I would some-day speak to large groups of people and that I would be involved in church-related ministry. My first job in a church was not as a preacher—it was as a janitor! I volunteered and was handed a broom and a dust cloth. I took on the chore of sweeping the church building and dusting the pews. The first people in the church with whom I shared the gospel were babies in the nursery. I'd pray over them and speak the love of God as I was changing their diapers.

The first people to whom I spoke on a regular basis were students in the classrooms where I was a teacher. The first people I counseled spiritually were the mothers of children in the inner-city projects where I was volunteering my time—I mostly was telling them how to prepare more nutritious meals for their children, how to take care of their daily needs, and how to keep their children from being influenced by gangs.

More than a decade after knowing deep in my heart that I would speak before large groups of people, I was finally handed a microphone.

Up until that moment I feel certain that countless people saw me as a young woman without resources—just another face in the crowd. They were right on that score—I was struggling and living in poverty. But I also knew that I was vitally connected spiritually to a God with unlimited resources and supply. I feel certain many people saw me as unqualified and without inner resources to speak publicly. On that score, they were wrong. I had been studying my Bible diligently for long hours every week. I knew what God had to say. I knew how to talk. I had a burning in me that was just waiting for the right time and place. When you prepare, God sends opportunity.

Never let anybody convince you that you do not have the resourcefulness or that you cannot obtain the resources to accomplish the dream in your heart. There's always a way if you are willing to seek it with single-minded purpose and a strong will to move up!

MOVING ON

How are you dealing with your critics?

MOVING UP

What more might you do to silence your critics
while maintaining your integrity?

18

The Changing Landscape of Your Path

Nance stared at the page of the photo album before her. "It's almost unbelievable how things have changed," she said. For her seventy-third birthday, her children and grandchildren had created this album as a tribute to her life. The particular page she was viewing had photos from a family reunion held sixty years ago.

The hairstyles and clothing styles were different, she noted, and also the make and model of the cars in the background of one photo. "We lived in a much different house then," she said, pointing to a house behind one group of relatives. "Nobody builds front porches and sidewalks these days. See the roof—no TV antenna because we didn't have television. See the water cooler—we didn't know about today's air-conditioning."

"Do you want to go back to the good old days?" one of her grandchildren asked, sensing nostalgia in her grandmother's voice.

"Good heavens, no!" Nance exclaimed. "I like these good *new* days. I'm just glad I survived the good old days to get to where I am now!"

Change is not limited to individual human beings. The environment changes. Society changes. Styles change. Technologies and systems and protocols change. As one person put it, "I'm not only a different person driving a different car, but the landscape along the way has changed."

Change is not limited to individual human beings. The environment changes. Society changes. Styles change.

NOT JUST TRAVELING—GOING SOMEWHERE!

There's an old question that many people in the South know. It's a question that tends to be asked if a person sees another person looking busy or acting important, but not necessarily accomplishing anything. The question is: "Are you just traveling... or are you going somewhere?"

I don't know about you, but I'm *going somewhere!*

I'm not the least bit interested in spinning my wheels. I'm not interested in busyness for the sake of busyness, or driving just for the sake of feeling the road or hearing the roar of my car's engine. I'm not interested in going through life as if I'm out on a casual meandering Sunday-afternoon drive along country roads. I have a destination to reach with the realization of the importance of the journey.

What about you?

Do you have a sense that the events of the past and present are leading you somewhere? Do you have an understanding of your destination, or your "destiny" (the inevitable succession of events)? Do you have an awareness that you are on God's path headed for a God-inspired goal?

Many people who are feeling pain, stretching, or hurt in transition don't have a clear understanding about which direction they are going or should go. They only know that they feel as if they were pushed into a blender and then somebody pushed the button that says "Frappe." They feel ripped apart and at the same time, life around them seems to be a blur.

Let me assure you that God is leading you somewhere. As you

trust in Him and yield to His processing of your life, you aren't just traveling—you are on a path toward the greatest joy, fulfillment, maturity, and purpose you have ever known.

YOUR UNIQUE LIFE IS ON A UNIQUE PATH

A path is a means between where you are and where you are to go. It is a journey through time and space. Your path involves places, seasons, and situations.

God's path leads you to your purpose. The purpose never changes. The landscape along the way may change dramatically. You may find yourself in a city you had never heard about, working for an enterprise you didn't know existed. You may find yourself in a remote area where you never thought you could survive. You may find yourself dramatically pulled from your current comfort zone into an area that somehow comes to feel more like home than anything you've ever known.

The specific path God calls you to walk will be uniquely your own. God will lead you to specific places, put you in specific organizations where you will fulfill specific roles, and give you specific opportunities that enable you to use fully the talents He has given you.

Although the path is unique to your life, it is not a path that you ever walk alone. God always walks with you, and all along the way—at various seasons and places and times—He puts others alongside you to walk where you are walking.

Although the path is unique to your life, it is not a path that you ever walk alone. God always walks with you.

I cannot predict or prophesy to you your particular path, but I do know three things about the paths God established for us.

1. The Path God Leads Each of Us to Walk Is Marked by Righteousness

God will never push us away or cause us to move into an evil realm—not for any reason or at any time. God does not tempt people to sin. He does not cause people to stray. He does not lead you in a wrong direction.

God desires to remain in right relationship with you at all times. That is the meaning of the word *righteousness*. The person in right standing will continue to do the right things in the right ways to stay in right standing with God.

The psalmist prayed that God would put light on his path so that he would not stumble, fall, or go astray. Prophets called for people to "make straight" the way of God—to remove all obstacles from their path that might keep them from walking precisely where and how God had directed them to walk.

It is up to us to choose to pursue a path marked by righteousness. We make this choice with our free will. We must say as often as necessary, "I choose to walk the path God has set before me."

2. The Path God Leads Each of Us to Walk Will Be Clearly Defined and Well Ordered

We are well acquainted with the phrase "law and order." God is the author of both.

One of the great examples of law and order is found in the book of Nehemiah. After the walls and gates of Jerusalem were rebuilt and repaired, a scribe named Ezra brought scrolls of the law before all the people and he read aloud to them and divided the people into groups under appointed leaders to learn the "sense" of what had been read and to cause the people to "understand the reading" (Neh. 8:8).

In this way, the rule of God's law or His principles was reestablished for God's people. The path of obedience was clearly defined and set before them.

The path God leads you to walk will never be a path that does not lead in some way toward the "living out" of God's laws and principles. He requires that the way we live be in alignment with what we say, what we believe, and the goals we seek to accomplish. The ends do not justify the means—good ends must be pursued by good means.

As a part of establishing order, God identifies His people clearly and gives them clearly bordered responsibilities. In the days of Nehemiah and Ezra, the people who qualified to live and work in Jerusalem were identified, numbered, and given the responsibility to contribute specific items or services to the functioning of God's temple.

This will happen in your life as well. God will help you, as you seek His help, to identify those who "belong" in your life.

God will help you, as you seek His help, to identify those who "belong" in your life.

Sometimes a person may be called upon by God to end certain affiliations or withdraw from certain memberships. Sometimes a person may be asked to undertake new responsibilities for and with other people. Sometimes a person may be asked to set new priorities for his assets, or pursue new endeavors with new associations.

It comes as a great surprise to some people to learn that God cares deeply about their friendships and associations. God cares deeply about who you marry and about how you relate to your family members.

God desires for you to live a peaceful life, and a significant contributor to peace—or wholeness—is having balanced relationships and a life rooted in principle. A well-ordered life is one that allows for maximum flexibility, strength, and focus as a person moves into his or her God-ordained purpose.

Have you ever been out in the woods and lost sight of the marked path that you had intended to follow? There's an almost immediate moment of panic, especially if you look up and can't see any of the people you thought were hiking that particular trail with you. The best thing you can do is stand still and start yelling for help.

The same is true in life. If you suddenly discover that you can't see the people you know God wanted you to have in your life...can't see the edges of the path...or you can't look ahead and see where the path clearly goes, stop walking. Call out to God for direction and help. Ask God to reveal to you where you went wrong and to show you how to get back on His path for your life. Ask Him to send you someone who can help you.

If you continue to wander aimlessly, you will likely find yourself far afield from the path that leads to your purpose. Not only that, but if you continue to walk alone and remain lost, you will eventually find yourself in real danger.

3. The Path God Puts before Us Is Marked by Celebrations

I know countless people who think of God as being a stern, unsmiling judge who delights in punishing wrongdoers. The image God presents about Himself in His Word is anything but that. God desires to lead and bless His people in a way that gives them genuine pleasure. After Ezra read the Law to the people and they understood it, they repented before God with tears and sought God's forgiveness. They knew they had erred and they were sorry in the depths of their heart for having done so. God sent this word through His leaders:

This day is holy unto the LORD your God; mourn not, nor weep. For all the people wept, when they heard the words of the law.

Then he said unto them, Go your way, eat the fat, and drink the sweet, and send portions unto them for whom nothing is prepared: for this day is holy unto our LORD: neither be ye sorry; for the joy of the LORD is your strength.

So the Levites stilled all the people, saying, Hold your peace, for the day is holy; neither be ye grieved.

And all the people went their way to eat, and to drink, and to send portions, and to make great mirth, because they had understood the words that were declared unto them. (Nehemiah 8:9–12)

In the immediate aftermath of this, God led Ezra and the other leaders to reinstitute the feast of tabernacles—a wonderful festival of thanksgiving and celebration that lasted seven days. On the eighth day, they had a solemn assembly of recommitting themselves to serving God.

As you walk the path God puts before you, you will encounter times when you are wise to face up to your sins and errors, the places you have "missed the mark," and to confess them to God and be forgiven. You will be wise to change your ways so you do not sin further. And you will encounter times when it is God's highest and best for you to celebrate His presence in your life, and to celebrate what you have accomplished that is in accordance with His plan for all mankind.

As you walk the path God puts before you, you will
encounter times when you are wise to face up to your
sins and errors, the places you have "missed the mark,"
and to confess them to God and be forgiven.

I admit to you that working is sometimes easier than partying. We feel justified when we are working long hours and with concentrated effort at tasks we believe are important. We feel a little guilty when we relax or celebrate, perhaps thinking that we are being self-indulgent or lazy. God made us, however, for celebration.

We might also be reluctant to celebrate because "partying" in our world today has taken on a connotation of worldliness and overindulgence in food, alcohol, and other substances or activities that are more associated with evil than with good. That does not need to be the case. Christians are some of the most fun-loving people I know. In fact, the most fun I've had in my life has been with Christians, doing simple things or playing simple games and choosing to see the funny side of ourselves and life in general.

Choose to take pleasure in the simple things of life. Stop to applaud a gorgeous sunset, to smell a beautiful rose, or enjoy a cold splash of spring water on your face. Stop to listen to the birds singing in your neighborhood as you go for an early morning walk.

Choose to laugh at your own foibles and flaws. Choose to laugh with, not at, others. Choose to be amused at the funny antics of children and animals at play.

Don't lose your sense of humor. Don't lose your sense of delight. God gave both of these to you for your enjoyment.

EVALUATE EVERY "DETOUR SIGN"

When my son was young, I liked to watch cartoons with him. Sometimes, a character would come upon a false detour sign. "Don't go, don't go!" we'd shout to the TV screen. We knew that the detour led straight over the edge of a cliff or into a trap of some kind.

As you walk the path God sets before you, the enemy of your soul will attempt to divert, diminish, or destroy you. He will put up "arguments" that amount to a false detour sign. We see this very clearly in Nehemiah's experience of rebuilding Jerusalem's walls.

The Detour Tactic of Mocking and Threatening

As stated in an earlier chapter, Nehemiah's enemies came first to him with open threats and mocking taunts—stop building now or face dire consequences. They called the Jews feeble, inept, overly ambitious but lazy, and foolish. Nehemiah answered by praying for God's help and then instituting a plan of combined defense and building—a strategy that was so brilliant it has been used for thousands of years since that day.

The enemy of your soul will tell you that you can't succeed in accomplishing God's goals for your life. He will mock you as weak, unqualified, unmotivated, and silly. Ignore the enemy! Keep your eyes on God, who not only created your path to success but also walks it with you.

The Detour Tactic of Proposed Compromise

When the tactic of threatening didn't stop Nehemiah's building campaign, Nehemiah's enemies sent an invitation to him, calling for Nehemiah, in essence, to "meet together to discuss options." You may encounter the same tactic.

Nehemiah's enemies invited him to come down from Jerusalem and meet with them on the plain of Ono. Nehemiah quickly discerned that they were out to destroy him.

Being out on an open plain would have made Nehemiah very vulnerable to attack. The name of this plain was also associated with compromise. Nehemiah knew that anything his enemies might seek to negotiate would leave Nehemiah weaker, not stronger.

Not all compromise results in weakness, but all compromise that detracts or subtracts from your accomplishing God's primary purposes for your life does make you weaker and, at the very least, delays your progress.

Nehemiah replied to this enemy invitation, "I am doing a great work, so that I cannot come down" (Neh. 6:3).

His enemies came with this invitation four times. Each time, Nehemiah responded to them in the same way. Many times your enemies know they cannot defeat you in a head-to-head confrontation, but they nonetheless hope to wear you out with anxiety and worry with their persistent nagging.

Many times your enemies know they cannot defeat you in a head-to-head confrontation, but they nonetheless hope to wear you out with anxiety and worry.

A few years ago a friend told me about a man whose wife had offered him "co-existence" rather than divorce. By that, she meant that he would have one end of the house to call his own, and she would have the other end of the house. They might meet for an occasional meal or evening of watching television together in the

living room, but for the most part, they would function indepen-
dently. Co-existence also meant that they would each have their
own funds, keep their own schedules, and pursue their own interests, with very little mutuality. The wife called this a "functional
marriage." Her husband responded, "No. I want a real marriage.
I want us to work on what is genuinely, truly a mutual life." She
walked out.

Their marriage was eventually reconciled, but at a tremendous
cost in money, emotional strain, and damaged relationships with
their children.

Some things are not to be compromised. Any suggestion that
you might compromise your character or integrity should be
refused without second thought. Any suggestion that you back
away from opportunities God has clearly placed into your hand
for the fulfillment of His good purposes in and through your life
should be refused immediately. Any suggestion that you should
abandon your responsibilities to your children should be refused
boldly. Any suggestion that you compromise your beliefs about
the truth of God's Word or the lordship of Jesus Christ should be
categorically refused with strong conviction.

Compromise is for matters of style and choices related to methodology. Compromise is not for matters involving deep commitments to God.

God's Word tells us that our responses in life should be yes or
no (James 5:12 *The Message*). We get ourselves into deep trouble
when we respond to our detractors with "maybe," "what if," and
"perhaps" negotiations that involve compromise of principle.

The Detour Tactic of False Accusations

When the tactic of proposed compromise didn't work, Nehemiah's
enemies came to him accusing him of having self-serving motives

that Nehemiah desired to keep secret. He responded, "There are no such things done as thou sayest" (Neh. 6:8). Enemies often come at us with lies about our virtue or questions about our motives. The best response is simply to say in the face of their false accusations, "That's a lie." We do ourselves little good by staying silent when others lie to us. We do not need to launch a major offensive or defensive campaign, but we should never let a lie stand. We need to call a lie and false claim for what it is.

Nehemiah knew that these accusations were an attempt to instill suspicion and, ultimately, fear. He prayed, "O God, strengthen my hands" (v. 9). "Hands," here, refers to an ability to produce or be productive, and strength is a sign of increased ability. Nehemiah prayed for an increase in productivity. He asked God to help him do more. What is your prayer?

In the face of accusations, resolve to strengthen your resolve!

The Detour Tactic of False Prophecy

When false accusations did not work, Nehemiah's enemies sent a man named Shemaiah, who was inside the walls of Jerusalem, to Nehemiah saying, "Let us meet together in the house of God, within the temple, and let us shut the doors of the temple: for they will come to slay thee; yea, in the night will they come to slay thee" (Neh. 6:10). Nehemiah refused to go. He perceived that God had not sent this man and that the word was a false prophecy inspired by his enemies. He knew that to go into hiding would send a signal to the people of the city that they were not secure and should be afraid. Nehemiah stood strong.

There may very well be well-meaning, even godly, people who will come to you in your pain and encourage you to withdraw from or to give up whatever ministry or good enterprises you have undertaken or established. They will entice you with a suggestion that this withdrawal is for your personal benefit and good, or for the good of the organization you have founded or led. Recognize that the signal you send if you do withdraw is a signal that in some way you are afraid, guilty, or lacking in commitment. Refuse to be tempted even by good people making good suggestions if their advice is not what God is saying to your heart, or is not the truth of God's Word.

Refuse to be tempted even by good people making good suggestions if their advice is not what God is saying to your heart, or is not the truth of God's Word.

Keep Building

All the while—through threats, offers of weakening compromise, false accusations, and false prophetic words—Nehemiah stayed close to God and the people continued to build. God's Word tells us that the wall was finished in what seemed to be record time—only fifty-two days! And moreover, the enemies of Nehemiah "were much cast down in their own eyes: for they perceived that this work was wrought of our God" (Neh. 6:16).

If you keep doing the work God has called you to do... the enemies who sought to stop you will be the ones who are stopped.

If you endure in pursuing your God-given purpose... your enemies will have their evil purposes completely thwarted.

If you persist in turning to God and refusing to give in to fear... your enemies will be forced to admit that God is on your side. With God on your side you will outlast your enemies!

Choose to Encourage Yourself—and to Stay Encouraged!

As far as I am concerned, one of the most encouraging verses in God's Word is Revelation 2:10. God spoke these words to the church that had been established in Smyrna, which was in the area we know as Turkey today. This church had already undergone severe tribulation, and had been the object of much ridicule and blasphemy from unbelievers. God said:

> Fear none of those things which thou shalt suffer: behold, the devil shall cast some of you into prison, that ye may be tried; and ye shall have tribulation ten days: be thou faithful unto death, and I will give thee a crown of life.

Note that God did not say to this church that He would keep them from further trouble. Rather, God said that the people in this church still had difficult days ahead. Some of them were going to be cast into prison. Even so, note that God said four extremely positive things in just this one brief sentence:

1. *"Fear none of those things which thou shalt suffer."* In other words, continue to be strong in your faith. Continue to trust God and believe His Word. There is no infamy in suffering. There is only infamy in refusing to believe.

2. *"That ye may be tried."* The purpose for the suffering was to be tested and refined. God fully expected those who were imprisoned to emerge from prison stronger than when they entered prison. Suffering does not give God information about our ability to believe or endure. Suffering informs *us* about the strength of God and our ability to believe and endure. There are some things God allows us to experience so that we will come to know what

we truly are made of. God wants you to know the strength of your commitment and the power of your faith.

3. "Ye shall have tribulation ten days." There is a set time for trouble and times of testing. All tribulation and pain comes to an end. Elsewhere in God's Word we read that God never tests us beyond our abilities (see 1 Cor. 10:13). If you are facing a problem, know that this problem *will* end.

4. "Be thou faithful." The word *faithful* literally means "full of faith." Faith is what gives a person enduring power. Faith is what conquers fear. And faith is what results in a "crown of life." Your faith will result in reward that produces all things beneficial for life and necessary for eternal life!

Faith is what gives a person enduring power.
Faith is what conquers fear.

MOVING ON

Have you encountered any false detour signs on the
path God has led you to walk?

MOVING UP

What are you doing to bolster your resolve to continue
walking the path God has prepared for you?

19

Gaining Strength through Perseverance

Nobody ever thought Joan would do what she did. She had always been the shy one in the group—the last to speak up, the first to withdraw into the shadows. After high school, she enrolled in a modeling course. Her family members and friends were stunned. "I want to gain some confidence," she said.

Her family members and friends were even more stunned when she took singing lessons. They had never heard her sing. "I like to sing," she said. "I want my voice to be stronger."

Her family members and friends were hugely stunned when she moved to Nashville and began to knock on doors seeking employment as a backup singer. She auditioned twenty-seven times before she was offered a small job. That was the beginning.

Over the next thirty years, Joan became one of the most successful backup singers in the recording industry. She never sought to be center stage. In fact, she never sought to be on stage at all. But she never gave up singing and never gave up trying new styles and new music. Much of her work involved singing backup for gospel soloists.

"What made you launch out like that?" her son asked her one day as they were talking about the early days of her career.

"I knew deep inside me that God had given me a voice and, son, whatever God gives you, you are supposed to use. I didn't start out strong, but I was determined to do what it would take to finish strong."

I like her statement as a definition for perseverance: doing what it takes to finish strong.

Most people I know want to be strong.

Most people I know hope they have enduring strength.

But most people I know also hope fervently that there is a way they can be strong and endure without having to put their perseverance to a test.

Nobody develops great strength or enduring power without coming against problems and pain, and outlasting them.

Nobody develops great strength or enduring power without coming against problems and pain, and outlasting them.

Perseverance is not a nicety or an option. It is a *must* if you are going to reach the place where you are living an authentic, purposeful, and fulfilling life. It is essential to moving on and up.

THREE OPPONENTS OF PERSEVERANCE

There are three things that work against perseverance. They are like "counter forces" that well up inside you as you strive to hold a steady, forward course. Those forces are perfectionism, temptation, and procrastination.

Perfectionism

Perseverance always comes against perfectionism. Most people think they are persevering in order to achieve perfection in their work or appearance. In truth, their desire for perfection nearly always undermines perseverance.

Perfectionists often don't want to pursue something that holds the potential for failure, or something that they fear they will not be able to do exceedingly well. In reality, the pursuit of any worthwhile goal takes the development of skills and the growth of personal character. All growing processes involve learning, and learning always involves a degree of error and failure. We make mistakes...so we might learn what *not* to do. We fall down when we are learning to walk...but in the process, we learn how to get up and try again. We learn incrementally, step by step, and in the process, we discover that diligent, frequent practice is required to perfect any skill, art, or performance ability.

In other cases, perfectionism keeps a person from finishing a project or crossing the finish line of a goal—the person seems incapable of releasing something because it doesn't seem good enough. Recognize this tendency if you have it. And accept the fact that nothing you or any other human being will ever do is perfect or can be perfect. We are all flawed in some way and we all make mistakes. We all produce work that can be improved. But if we refuse to contribute something to this world that is slightly less than perfect, we will contribute nothing to this world.

Certainly I am not advocating that a person do shoddy work or take a haphazard approach to things she undertakes. Far from it! I admire excellence, desire excellence, and attempt to produce excellence in everything I undertake. But I also know that only God is perfect, and only what God does can be 100 percent right, 100 percent of the time. Give yourself permission to be human.

Temptations

The enemy of your soul will always find ways to present to you enticing temptations to lead you astray into sin and error. The enemy of your soul knows your weakness and preys upon it. You can expect to be hit with all sorts of negative thoughts about your own ability and suitability. You can expect to be hit with all sorts of seemingly positive options that provide a faster or easier way toward reaching your goals.

Temptations are not always enticements to do evil. Sometimes they are enticements that are innocent and even fun. A new hobby, an interesting friendship, an intriguing opportunity can keep you from staying on course and persevering toward your goal just as much as an enticement to be disobedient or rebellious. Always remember that good is the worst enemy of best.

Procrastination

Every person is prone to a degree of procrastination—a reluctance to begin. We may procrastinate in starting a project, making a phone call, going to the place we know we must go, or even getting up in the morning. Procrastination is a mild form of laziness or slothfulness. It is saying, "I can wait on this." In truth, the longer you wait to start something you know is beneficial for your life, the more difficult it will be for you to take the first step.

In truth, the longer you wait to start something you know is beneficial for your life, the more difficult it will be for you to take the first step.

CONFRONT THE OBSTACLES

Not only do perfectionism, temptations, and procrastination keep us from persevering, but they create obstacles in our path that require time, energy, and sometimes money to remove. They force us to persevere in the removal of an obstacle so that we can persevere in walking forward on God's path.

Every plan and every path is subject to a certain degree of alterations, the exercise of different options, and a degree of editing or revision. These things fall into the category of "outside" forces over which we often have no control or influence.

I have learned this in countless ways, one of which is in the writing of books. What I first write is never exactly what appears in print. Many times when I read my own words, I recognize that there is more I wanted to say, or perhaps that I would be wise to say less than what I have said. Even when I am satisfied that my message is clearly stated and adequate, my words are subjected to editors, who both raise questions and correct errors.

I have also learned that life doesn't play fair or always turn out the way a person attempts to script life. Very often, we encounter obstacles that are actually the resistance or reluctance of people who are close to us who do not want us (whether intentionally or unintentionally) to continue walking the path God has set before us. This is not to place blame on another person but to say life often puts us at a crossroads.

I have personally had to face this in many different ways. I have experienced those endless nights of lying on a floor crying until I could not cry anymore, wanting to eat but could not eat, knowing I was wasting away to nothing. I have wondered if there would ever be a time I would laugh again, love again, or even feel again. I have faced extreme disorientation as I forged to find what was "real" and what was not. Some situations were not direct resis-tance or opposition of others, but some simply the "yuck" side of life. I have hurt beyond measure while standing strong in faith, through disease and death of a loved one. I have felt helpless to fix or make better the pain of those I care for who suffer greatly. I know and understand the perplexities of everything in your life changing, without your activation in it.

You cannot always have things your way. As we've seen, you can't control everything:

- You cannot demand that a person love you. You cannot stop a person from rejecting you.
- You cannot force a customer to buy your product. You cannot keep out all thieves, embezzlers, or intruders, no matter how hard you may try.
- You cannot predict world markets or international affairs with precision. You cannot predict tomorrow's scientific breakthrough or technological advance—which may make your life or product or service obsolete or less attractive.
- You cannot stop the advancement of time or put a complete stop to the aging process. You cannot prevent all disease or eliminate the certainty of death.

All you *can* do is pursue your goal with as much energy, effort, and wisdom as possible—asking always for God's guidance. All you *can* do is believe for the best, and be sensitive to changes and quickly adapt to them.

There is little we can do to avoid the obstacles that are created by others or by life.

What we can avoid, however, are the obstacles that come as the result of our own perfectionism, yielding to temptation, or procrastination. In sum, don't create problems for yourself. Sufficient to the path are the obstacles and problems that come from outside yourself!

Don't Compound a Problem

Be aware that temptations, detours, and procrastination become even more detrimental when obstacles appear in your path. It is in the presence of a profound obstacle that a person is much more likely to be enticed to do things that actually make the obstacle more prominent or difficult.

Be aware that temptations, detours, and procrastination become even more detrimental when obstacles appear in your path.

Is your marriage difficult? That's not the time to turn to alcohol or drugs or overeating or overspending and become addicted to them. Substances or unhealthy forms of escape will not remove the obstacle or help you overcome it. Addiction will only create a bigger and more difficult obstacle.

Have you suffered storm damage to property important for your housing or business? That's not the time to turn to a cheap "fix." In the long run, inadequate repair is likely to create an even bigger headache for you, and greatly thwart your ability to resell your home or business property later.

Has your business partner decided to bail out? That is not the time to fall to pieces or offer greater incentives for your partner to stay involved. If the person wants out, the person will eventually get out—sooner or later. Get busy finding a way to buy out your partner and move forward. Or, take on a new partner who can help your business grow.

Let me also caution you about "small" obstacles. We often try to overlook the little stones in our path, perhaps hoping they will go away, or perhaps thinking they aren't worthy of our notice. Sometimes it is the small issue that becomes a pebble in our shoe—it keeps us from walking boldly and with maximum flexibility.

I'm not referring to petty annoyances encountered in a particular transaction, or to the mood swings of any given day—either your mood swings or those of others around you. I'm referring to habitual, frequent, or ongoing insults, threats, unfounded criticism, unreasonable demands, or behavior that seems on a downward spiral into deep discouragement or depression. Don't let those factors in your relationships go unchallenged or unaddressed. Insist that a person get help or go with you to get help. No person can be their creative best, or achieve their highest goals, if they are continually sideswiped with ridicule, threats, or impossible demands.

Don't Give Up

Obstacles in your path do not mean the end to your journey. Obstacles can nearly always be tunneled under, bypassed, or climbed over. The decision you must make is to find a way to continue to move forward, and to refuse to sit down in the shadow of an obstacle and quit.

THREE CLOSE COUSINS OF PERSEVERANCE

Perseverance has three close cousins: patience, discipline, and the ability to admit an error and change course.

The Character Trait of Patience

Patience is part of perseverance. God's Word tells us: "Behold, the husbandman waiteth for the precious fruit of the earth, and hath long patience for it, until he receive the early and latter rain. Be ye also patient; stablish your hearts" (James 5:7–8).

Patience is the ability to wait for a desired result without becoming annoyed, upset, or provoked to anger. In many ways, patience is a conserving of your energy and focus. If you allow yourself to become annoyed, upset, anxious, frustrated, or angry about the seemingly slow progress or growth, you will dissipate precious energy that is better applied to producing something positive.

Discipline to Stay the Course

Most of life's greatest achievements are not the result of flashes of intellectual brilliance or bursts of superhuman strength. Most of life's greatest achievements come at the end of long, arduous, persistent effort. A scientist may have dozens of "no results" experiments before the successful experiment that produces a beneficial medication. A musician may try dozens of musical motifs before hitting upon a certain sequence and rhythm of notes that becomes a hit song. A student will have to persevere through dozens of courses to earn a desired degree. A farmer will make dozens of passes through a field—weeding, cultivating, applying fertilizer and insecticides—before that final pass that brings in the harvest.

Most disciplines involve repetition or habit. How do you decide which disciplines to fold into your life? How do you decide which habits are worth developing? First, envision how you want to live your life in the future. What kind of health do you want? What kind of relationships do you want? What kind of activity do you want? What kind of income or resources do you want? Then, determine what is necessary for you to have that life. Identify the daily habits that will produce, over time, the results you want. Manage your schedule to make sure those disciplines are part of each day.

Wisdom to Change Course When Necessary

Are there ever goals that are not worthy of further pursuit? Certainly. Any goal we set for ourselves that is not in keeping with God's Word or God's personal design for our lives is not a goal we should pursue. If we recognize that we are walking down a path that does not lead us toward the fulfillment of God's plan and purpose for our lives, we need to find the path that *does* lead to that fulfillment. It doesn't matter how long we may have been walking the wrong path — or the commitments we may have made to fellow human beings along the way. We must put ourselves into alignment with God's design if we truly are going to experience the best and the highest life.

We must put ourselves into alignment with God's design if we truly are going to experience the best and the highest life.

Changing our course to obey God does not mean we lack perseverance. It means we have wisdom to make the adjustment necessary so that we can move more directly toward our God-authorized purpose.

THE BREAKTHROUGH TO STRENGTH

As you persevere, you eventually come to a breakthrough that results in genuine strength. I can't explain how this happens, or predict precisely when it may happen, but I know it happens. I have experienced it on countless occasions.

Suddenly, obstacles that were formidable seem to dissipate.

Suddenly, things that were difficult become easier.

Suddenly, things that caused pain no longer hurt.

When I work out in a gym, I chase pain. That is the opposite of the way many people exercise. I have watched people in gyms who work out until they begin to feel pain or exhaustion. They stop the moment they feel discomfort. The net result is that they do not become stronger. They may be expending a few calories, but they are not truly strengthening the muscles of their body.

When I work with weights or run, I pursue pain. I want to get to that moment when I don't think I can run another step or do one more crunch or do one more repetition, and then, I *do* run another step, do one more crunch, or do one more repetition. I know that it is in moving through the pain and continuing on that I truly am gaining strength.

Whatever you do, do it to the utmost of your ability.

Press against your personal best.

Test your limits.

The breakthrough will come that results in greater confidence and force of character. When you refuse to break, bow, or bend...you will grow in personal power.

Therefore...

Keep doing what you have been called to do.

Keep standing.

Keep working.

Keep pursuing the goals God has set before you.

The ability to finish is evidence of the ability to endure.
Keep moving on!
Keep moving up!
That's the key to turning yesterday's trials into today's triumphs!

MOVING ON

What are you enduring today?
In what areas of your life are you persevering?

MOVING UP

How do you motivate yourself to continue persevering?

About the Author

Paula White, co-founder of Without Walls International Church in Tampa, Florida, is a renowned life coach, bestselling author, and highly sought-after motivational speaker.

Paula launched her television show, *Paula Today,* in 2001 and immediately captivated the attention of the American audience. Her viewership soon grew to international prominence due to her ability to connect with people from diverse backgrounds. She has been tagged by the media as "Dr. Phil meets Mother Teresa." Paula has an uncanny ability to reach out in a very real and relevant manner with a heart of compassion, teaching others life principles and success strategies, and at the same time to empower individuals to fulfill their destiny.

Although her early childhood was marred by her father's suicide and her innocence was stolen by intermittent sexual and physical abuse between the ages of six and thirteen, Paula refuses to be labeled a victim. She continues to press toward the mark of her high calling and has dedicated her life to pulling others out of their crippling circumstances. Each year she sponsors large-scale outreaches to touch the lives of the less fortunate, offering hope and encouragement along with practical life-application solutions. "To hold on to your dream and fulfill God's plan for your life, you must keep moving forward," says Paula.

Today, in addition to hosting her daily television show reaching a potential worldwide viewing audience of 2.3 billion people, Paula is a contributor for a number of TV programs and magazines, coaching others through important life issues. Her commitment to humanity is felt around the globe as she reaches out through charities and compassion ministries, always staying true to her core goal of transforming lives, healing hearts, and winning souls.

If you enjoyed
Move On, Move Up

look for *Dare to Dream*, another life-changing book by Paula White!

Paula White is here to dare you to dream! As a woman who has experienced tragedy and triumph, poverty and prosperity, Paula is uniquely qualified to share powerful insights with those who desire a better life and a stronger sense of self. Paula writes out of her own painful experiences and reveals the keys to healing, hope, and identity. You were not created to be shackled by negative emotions or memories. You were created to live a bold, dynamic, creative life filled with love and joy!

Through real-life illustrations, personal stories, and stirring insights, Paula shows you how to:

- See yourself through new eyes
- Move beyond loss
- Shake off painful memories, worries, fears, and failures
- Take control of what you think, say, and believe
- Establish new boundaries
- Embrace a lifetime of discovery and transformation

If you are willing to do those things, one step at a time, you are on the road to victory!

Available June 2009
wherever books are sold